The Basics o

Should I say 'He is taller than I' or 'He is taller than me?'

Do you spell it 'blond' or 'blonde'?

If you've ever been stopped in your tracks by questions like these, then this book is for you. A complete pocket guide to the ins and outs of everyday English, *The Basics of English Usage* will tell you all you need to know about such topics as:

- Correct spelling
- Good grammar and style
- Punctuation and how to use it
- Problem words that everyone gets wrong

The Basics of English Usage is an indispensable survival guide for anyone wanting to improve their writing and communication.

Wynford Hicks is a freelance journalist and editorial trainer. He has worked as a reporter, subeditor, feature writer, editor and editorial consultant in magazines, newspapers and books. He is the author of *Quite Literally* and *English for Journalists*, now in its third edition.

WYNFORD HICKS

The Basics of English Usage

Routledge
Taylor & Francis Group

LONDON AND NEW YORK

First published 2009
by Routledge
2 Park Square, Milton Park, Abingdon, Oxon, OX14 4RN

Simultaneously published in the USA and Canada
by Routledge
270 Madison Avenue, New York, NY 10016

Routledge is an imprint of the Taylor & Francis Group

© 2009 Wynford Hicks

Typeset in Rotis by
Keystroke, 28 High Street, Tettenhall, Wolverhampton
Printed and bound in Great Britain by
CPI Antony Rowe, Chippenham, Wiltshire

British Library Cataloguing in Publication Data
A catalogue record for this book is available from the British Library

Library of Congress Cataloging in Publication Data
A catalog record for this book has been requested

ISBN 10: 0-415-47023-4 (pbk)
ISBN 13: 978-0-415-47023-0 (pbk)

Contents

Contents

Introduction

Why bother learning the rules of grammar? Who cares about punctuation? Why waste your time learning how to spell when every word-processing program on every computer is equipped with spell-check?

Back in the 1960s educationists and teachers revolted against what they called the straitjacket of correct English. They claimed that learning the rules was pointless because there was no evidence that knowing them improved students' writing. And in any case they objected to many of the rules on the grounds that they were irrelevant, out of date and elitist.

Since then there has been a return to common sense. The orthodox view in the classroom is once again that learning the rules of standard English is an essential part of being educated. There is also a welcome stress on the importance of context in determining whether and to what extent the rules should be followed.

In a history essay or an English exam, a written application for a job, a letter of complaint to the local council, it's appropriate to write in standard English. This is a formal setting. Your carefully chosen style makes what you say accessible to strangers, whereas an informal, casual, slangy approach would draw attention to itself, obscure the message, risk confusion.

By contrast, in a text message or email to a friend who shares your background and vocabulary you can relax and write without straining to be formal. There's nothing new here, after all. All sorts of people, including successful writers, have often written letters to one another using abbreviations, private code, eccentric punctuation – not the sort of thing you would expect to see in their published work.

But learning the rules and conventions of standard English is essential if you plan to follow a career where this is expected or if you want to take part in public life; not to learn them is to restrict yourself to a marginal role in society.

Introduction

This is a practical book about using English, not a theoretical one about analysing it. So it uses the traditional terms of dictionaries and usage guides rather than the technical ones of linguistics textbooks. You'll find 'nouns' and 'verbs' here rather than 'morphemes' and 'phonemes'.

There is a simple reason for this. Let's assume we're trying to decide which of the following forms we might use and which we might not:

1 He is taller than I.
2 He is taller than me.
3 He is taller than I am.
4 He (is) taller than me am.

Beyond the observation that nos 2 and 3 are familiar and seem acceptable to most people, while no 1 is stilted/archaic and no 4 is unheard of (except possibly in an Afro-Caribbean dialect), what can we say? On what basis is 'than' followed by 'me' in 2 but by 'I' in 3? If we use the traditional terms of grammar, then we can explain things as follows: 'than' is a preposition in 2 (it comes before the pronoun 'me') but a conjunction in 3 (it links two clauses, each of which has a subject and a verb). A preposition takes the objective case ('to her' not 'to she') whereas a conjunction is followed by the subjective case ('I' not 'me' is the subject of 'am').

Traditional grammatical terms have several advantages, including the fact that they often correspond to terms in other languages. In French, for example, an adjective is an *adjectif*, a noun is a *nom* and a verb is a *verbe*. It's beyond the scope of this book to make suggestions about learning other languages but there's no doubt that it helps to start with a grasp of the grammar of your own – and some idea about grammar in general.

This book is written in standard English – and takes it for granted that having a standard form is a good idea. Some academic language experts claim that standard English is not necessarily more logical or elegant than its dialects. But most of them would agree with this statement by RL Trask:

> It is simply *convenient* to have a standard form of the language which is agreed on by everybody ... Like a standard electrical plug, like a standard videotape, like a standard size for car tyres, standard English is valuable because it *is* standardised.

Between the two most influential forms of standard English – British and American – there are important differences, eg in spelling, which are discussed in this book. But the similarities between the two are in some ways more striking.

That or Which, and Why, an American handbook by Evan Jenkins published in 2007, contains little for the British to disagree with. For example, Jenkins says that ' "different from" is preferable to "different than" '; that 'due to' shouldn't be used to mean 'because of'; and that 'lay' (transitive) should be distinguished from 'lie' (intransitive) – so you lay the table but lie down on the bed. And he has critical things to say about words like 'decimate', 'impact' as a verb and 'utilise' (though of course he spells it 'utilize').

The subtitle of Jenkins' book, *A Usage Guide for Thoughtful Writers and Editors*, puts it in the tradition of HW Fowler's classic *Modern English Usage*, revised by RW Burchfield. Jenkins discusses various points of grammar but his book is, rightly, not described as a 'grammar'. It's more than that because it interprets, argues and revises rather than merely stating and explaining 'the rules'.

In this book 'grammar' – the rules and conventions that are the basis of a language – is combined with 'style', an altogether looser notion that has to do with the way in which somebody writes. And the Grammar and style chapter is organised alphabetically rather than by topic. This is to help you find what you're looking for, since some people disagree about what is and what isn't 'grammar' and others aren't familiar with the basic terms needed to explain it.

Take the split infinitive ('to boldly go'), for example. Is it 'bad grammar' or 'bad style' – or not something to bother about at all? Can you end a sentence with a preposition or start one with a conjunction? Should 'can' in that last sentence be 'may' or 'should'? Can/should 'you' in that sentence be 'one'? And so on.

The Grammar and style chapter tries to answer questions like these, offering practical advice. But it does not pretend to give definitive answers that will stand for all time. Compared with the relatively straightforward ones on spelling and punctuation, the chapter on grammar and style contains more advice which can be disputed – and may well need to be revised in the future.

The same is true of the chapter on problem words, since words and people's attitudes to them are constantly changing. New problems emerge as old ones disappear. Yesterday's blunder is today's cliché.

It's impossible to say exactly how the grammar, style and vocabulary of English will change in the future – but one thing looks certain. There will always be a need for a standard form of the language so that people can understand each other.

1
Spelling

English spelling is easy to make fun of – and not easy to get right. It certainly defies logic. We spell 'harass' with one 'r' and 'embarrass' with two; the noun 'dependant' has an 'a' in the last syllable while the adjective 'dependent' has an 'e'. In British English we spell 'licence' and 'practice' with a 'c' when they're nouns and with an 's' when they're verbs ('she has a licence to practise'; 'they licensed the practice') – though we pronounce them in exactly the same way. In American English, on the other hand, 'license' with an 's' does for both noun and verb – and so does 'practice' with a 'c'. Confused?

The numerals 'four' and 'fourteen' are followed by 'forty' – suddenly the 'u' has disappeared although the pronunciation of 'four' and 'for' by most people is the same. 'Mantelpiece', the shelf covering the fire, shows its Latin origin (*mantellum*, cloak) more clearly than 'mantle', the word actually used to mean 'cloak'. 'Metal' in its literal sense of iron or steel differs from 'mettle' meaning 'courage', as does 'flower', the general term for what plants produce, from 'flour', the particular 'flower' derived from wheat. And so on . . .

It's claimed that there are more than 200 ways of spelling the 40-odd distinct sounds in English. For example, Bill Bryson (in *Mother Tongue*, 1990) says there are 14 ways of conveying the 'sh' sound, as in *shoe, sugar, passion, ambitious, ocean, champagne*; more than a dozen for 'o', as in *go, beau, stow, sew, doe, though, escargot*; and another dozen for 'a', as in *hey, stay, make, maid, freight, great*. Including proper nouns, the English word with the greatest number of variants is said to be *air* with 38, as in *Aire, Ayr, heir, e'er, ere* . . .

The primary explanation for this rich confusion lies in the history of English. Unlike French, say, or German, English is a mongrel language – an amalgam of Anglo-Saxon and Old Norse, Norman French and Latin, which went on to adopt and absorb words and idioms from all over the world. The Anglo-Saxon of the Germanic invaders of the fifth century AD evolved in various regional dialects and spellings and was strongly influenced by the next wave of invaders, the Vikings, who spoke a related but different language, Old Norse. Then in 1066 came the Norman Conquest.

Suddenly England was a bilingual country (or a trilingual one if you include church Latin). The ruling class of nobles and clerics spoke a northern dialect of French while the peasants talked Anglo-Saxon among themselves. Slowly the two languages came together and when the bilingual period was over, English had absorbed much French vocabulary, spelling and pronunciation. More than a third of the English words in a modern dictionary are said to come from French.

Because of its complex history, English spelling is a mixture of different influences: Roman missionaries writing down Old English for the first time; Norman French scribes with their own ideas (replacing cw by qu to produce queen – which looks like a French word but isn't); and the growth of different dialects in different parts of the country. But the introduction of printing in the fifteenth century had the biggest impact of all. When William Caxton set up his printing house in London in 1476, he started publishing in the East Midlands dialect, used at court, in the universities of Oxford and Cambridge and in London. This brought a degree of standardisation.

Gradually during the next century the idea of standard spelling became popular. There were radical reformers like John Hart, who wrote several books advocating substantial change to achieve consistency, and practical pedagogues like Richard Mulcaster, a headmaster who wrote his own book, the *Elementarie* (1582), arguing that piecemeal reform was a more prudent course of action – things had gone too far for radical change. Mulcaster created an alphabetical list of over 8,500 words with recommended spellings, based on what he saw people using in their handwritten texts.

Early in the eighteenth century there was a proposal to establish an English academy on the lines of the Académie Française, founded in 1635, to police the language generally and lay down standards for spelling. Although it was supported by the Royal Society, by eminent writers like Dryden, Evelyn and Swift – and even by the government in 1712 – nothing happened. Several dictionaries were published in this period, notably one by Nathaniel Bailey (1721), but it was Samuel Johnson's magisterial *Dictionary of the English Language* (1755) that established a standard English spelling, much of which is in use today.

Johnson is sometimes described as 'creating' a standard spelling – but in his preface he explicitly rules this out: 'Even in words of which the derivation is apparent, I have been often obliged to sacrifice uniformity to custom.' As Philip Howard noted (in *The State of the Language*, 1984): 'Johnson followed the spelling generally adopted by the printers, establishing it in private use as the standard of literate English writers and spellers.'

Johnson's American equivalent, Noah Webster (1758–1843), was also credited with more than he tried to achieve. He didn't set out to change American but to systematise it and establish it as of equal status to English. If sales are any guide, he certainly succeeded: his American *Spelling Book* (1788) was so popular it had sold 60 million copies by 1890.

The curious thing is that in the book Webster explicitly rejected the spelling that seems today the most typically American: the dropping of the 'u' from words like 'honour' and 'favour'. He wrote that some of his fellow Americans had 'omitted the letter that is sounded, and retained one that is silent; for the words are pronounced *onur, favur*'. But he did include 'honor' and 'color' as variant spellings in his great *American Dictionary of the English Language* (1828) and they gradually became standard American.

Most of the other characteristic American spellings,* like '-er' where the British write '-re', as in centre and kilometre, and the

---

* For a summary of American spelling rules and examples of American spellings see 'American spelling', p. 28.

single 'p' where the British write 'pp', as in worshipped and kid-napper, were first recorded by Webster. He didn't impose them: they were fixed by usage not precept. His main contribution to American English was to give it the courage of its own convictions.

Webster was also a passionate spelling reformer and he was not alone. In the United States Benjamin Franklin, Mark Twain and Andrew Carnegie; in Britain Charles Darwin, Alfred Tennyson, Conan Doyle, James Murray (the first editor of the *Oxford English Dictionary*) and George Bernard Shaw all supported spelling reform. Isaac Pitman, the inventor of a shorthand system based on phonetic principles, joined the movement. Reform associations appeared on both sides of the Atlantic. But nothing came of it all.

The argument against spelling reform was and is very simple. Since English words are spoken in so many different ways, how could it be possible to reform spelling in the direction of speech? Whose speech?

It remains to be seen whether the computer and the internet will succeed where the spelling reformers failed. Certainly there are signs of standardisation in international printing and an increase in American spelling in books published for the international market. In 1992 the International Labour Office, which is based in Geneva, revised its house style and replaced the 's' of, for example, standardise with the American 'z' (traditionally favoured by the Oxford University Press). But over the past 20 years the 'z' has lost ground in Britain. The *Times* (the only British newspaper which previously insisted on retaining it) and various publishers have abandoned it.

Words people get wrong

First, here's a list of words that many people can't spell. How about you?

abhorrence
accidentally
accommodation
acquiescence
admissible
annihilate
apartment
apostasy
asinine
asphyxiate
authoritative
auxiliary

benefited
blamable
braggadocio
bureaucracy

Caribbean
clamouring
connoisseur
consensus
convertible
corpuscle
corroborate
crucifixion

debatable
definitely
descendant
desiccated
destructible
diagrammatic
diarrhoea
dignitary
discernible
dispel
dissatisfaction
dysentery

ecstasy
effervescence
eligibility
embarrass
emissary
exaggerate
exhilaration
expatriate

fallacious
forty
fulfilling
funereal

gaseous
guttural

haemorrhage
harass
heinous
herbaceous
hiccup
hierarchy
humorous
hygiene
hysterical

ideologist
idiosyncrasy
impresario
indispensable
indissoluble
innocuous
innuendo
inoculate
instalment
intestacy
iridescence

jeopardise

kitchenette

liaison
licentious
linchpin
liquefy
loquacious

maintenance
manoeuvre
mantelpiece
mayonnaise
meanness
Mediterranean
mellifluous
millennium
miniature
minuscule
miscellaneous
mischievous
moccasin

negotiate
nonchalant
noticeable

obeisance
occurred
omitted
oscillate

paraphernalia
pavilion
perspicacious
plummeted
predilection
privilege
profession
proprietary
pseudonym
publicly

pursue	targeted
Pyrenees	tranquillity
rarefy	unforeseen
recommend	unnecessary
reconnaissance	unparalleled
referred	
restaurateur	vacillate
resuscitate	verruca
riveted	veterinary
	vociferous
sacrilegious	
separate	withhold
statutory	
straitjacket	
supersede	

Confusions

One reason why people misspell some words is that they confuse them with other words. There are three common kinds of confusion:

1   A word is confused with a shorter one that sounds the same:

coconut – cocoa
consensus – census
dispel – spell
fulfil – full/fill
minuscule – mini
playwright – write
supersede – cede

2   A word is confused with a different one that sounds the same (homophone):

altar – alter
aural – oral
bail – bale
bait – bate
born – borne
breach – breech
cannon – canon
complement – compliment
cord – chord
counsel – council
curb – kerb
currant – current
deserts (runs away/what is deserved) – desserts (puddings)
draft – draught
discreet – discrete
faze – phase
forbear – forebear
forego – forgo
foreword – forward
formally – formerly
geezer – geyser
grisly – grizzly
hanger – hangar
horde – hoard
lead (the metal) – led (the past participle)
lightening – lightning
metal – mettle
principal – principle
raise – raze
review – revue

sight – site
stationary – stationery
storey – story
swat – swot
toe – tow
way – weigh
yoke – yolk

3   A word used as one part of speech is confused with the same word used as another part of speech:

Noun
practice
Verb
practise, *so also* practising, practised
Noun
licence
Verb
license, *so also* licensing, licensed
Noun
envelope
Verb
envelop, *so also* enveloping, enveloped
Noun
dependant
Adjective
dependent

Only in 'envelop' / 'envelope' are the two words pronounced differently:

Noun – *en*velope
Verb – en*ve*lop

Spelling

If you find it difficult to distinguish between the common pairs *practic(s)e* and *licenc(s)e*, note that *advic(s)e* changes its pronunciation as well as spelling and remember the three pairs together:

Noun
advice
Verb
advise
Noun
practice
Verb
practise
Noun
licence
Verb
license

Or remember the sentence:

Doctors need a licence to practise.

In this case the noun ('c') comes before the verb ('s').

Also note the opposite problem: two words with the same spelling that are pronounced differently and have different meanings:

*in*valid (as in chair)
in*valid* (as in argument)

de*serts* (runs away, what is deserved)
*de*serts (sand)

lead (the metal)
lead (the present tense)

re*ject* (verb)
*re*ject (noun)

pro*ject* (verb)
*pro*ject (noun)

I before e

Most people know the spelling rule 'i' before 'e' except after 'c'. This gives:

believe, niece, siege

and

ceiling, deceive, receive

But note that the rule applies only to the 'ee' sound and that there are exceptions such as:

caffeine, codeine, counterfeit, protein, seize

And, in the other direction:

species

Plurals

1   Nouns ending in a consonant followed by 'y' take 'ies' in the plural:

lady – ladies
penny – pennies
story – stories

But proper nouns take the standard 's' in the plural:

the two Germanys
three Hail Marys
four Pennys in a class list

And nouns ending in a vowel followed by 'y' take the standard 's' in the plural:

donkey – donkeys
monkey – monkeys
storey – storeys

2   Most nouns ending in 'o' take the standard 's' but some common ones take 'es' in the plural:

buffaloes, cargoes, dingoes, echoes, embargoes, goes, heroes, Negroes, potatoes, tomatoes, vetoes, volcanoes

And some may be spelt either with 's' or 'es':

archipelago, banjo, domino, grotto, halo, innuendo, mango, memento, mosquito, motto, no, salvo, tornado, torpedo

3   Nouns ending in 'f' usually take the standard 's' in the plural:

dwarf – dwarfs
handkerchief – handkerchiefs

(But 'dwarves' and 'handkerchieves' are found.)
Note:

elf – elves

4   Some nouns that come from Greek, Latin or modern languages
keep their original plural form:

addendum – addenda
alumna – alumnae
alumnus – alumni
bacillus – bacilli
château – châteaux
criterion – criteria
minimum – minima
phenomenon – phenomena
spectrum – spectra

In some cases both the original plural form and an anglicised version
are used:

appendix
appendices (used of books)
appendixes (used of both books and the body)

beau
beaux
beaus

Spelling

bureau
bureaux
bureaus

cactus
cacti
cactuses

formula
formulae (scientific)
formulas (general use)

fungus
fungi
funguses

index
indices (mathematics)
indexes (books)

medium
media (the press etc)
mediums (spiritualism)

memorandum
memoranda
memorandums

plateau
plateaux
plateaus

referendum
referenda
referendums

stadium
stadia
stadiums

syllabus
syllabi
syllabuses

terminus
termini
terminuses

virtuoso
virtuosi
virtuosos

Be careful of confusing the singular with the plural when the latter form is more common, as with:

graffito – graffiti
die – dice
stratum – strata

The plural of 'wagon-lit' is 'wagons-lits', not as some British dictionaries insist 'wagons-lit' or 'wagon-lits'; the plural of 'court martial' is 'courts martial'.

But note that plurals such as 'agenda', 'data' and 'media' are often treated as though they were singular.

Suffixes

1 One-syllable words with a short vowel and a single final consonant double it before a suffix that starts with a vowel:

fat – fatten, fatter
run – runner, running

2 So, too, do words with more than one syllable if the stress is on
the final syllable:

begin
beginning, beginner

refer
referred, referral

prefer
preferred – but note *preferable* (pronounced *pre*ferable)

3 But one-syllable words with a long vowel or double vowel do
not double the final consonant:

seat
seated, seating

look
looking, looked

4 Nor do words with more than one syllable if the stress is before
the final syllable:

*proff*er
proffering, proffered

*bene*fit
benefiting, benefited

*lea*flet
leafleting, leafleted

5 Exceptions to these rules include most words ending in '1':

cavil – cavilling
devil – devilled (but *devilish*)
level – levelled
revel – reveller
travel – traveller

but

parallel – paralleled

and some words ending in 'p' or 's':

worship – worshipped
bus – buses
gas – gases

while some words ending in 's' are optional:

bias – biased or biassed
focus – focused or focussed

6 Sometimes the stress changes when a noun is used as a verb:

format
formative but for*mat*ted (in computer speak)

Dictionaries generally give:

combat
combatant
combative
combated

But there is an argument for 'com*bat*ted' on the grounds that some people pronounce it that way. (You can, of course, avoid the problem altogether by using 'fight' as a verb instead of 'combat': it's slightly shorter.)

7   'Learn' can become 'learnt' or 'learned' in the past tense; 'dream' can become 'dreamt' or 'dreamed'. But 'earn' can only become 'earned'.

8   Words ending in a silent 'e' keep it if the suffix begins with a consonant:

safe – safety
same – sameness

But note that there are common exceptions:

due – duty
true – truly
awe – awful (but awesome)
wide – width

And some words are optional:

acknowledg(e)ment, judg(e)ment

9 Words ending in a silent 'e' drop it if the suffix begins with a vowel:

bake – baking
sane – sanity

but

change – changeable
mile – mileage

Note that 'y' here acts as a vowel:

gore – gory
ice – icy

10 Sometimes keeping or losing the silent 'e' makes it possible to distinguish two words with different meanings:

dying (the death)
dyeing (clothes)

linage (payment by the line)
lineage (descent)

singing (musically)
singeing (burning)

swinging (from a tree)
swingeing (heavy)

American spelling

The main differences between American and British spelling are:

1 doubling before a suffix: in words of more than one syllable ending in 'l' or 'p' American follows the general rule and does not double the consonant – traveler (instead of traveller), signaled (signalled), equaling (equalling), kidnaped (kidnapped), worshiping (worshipping);
2 but, confusingly, in some other words ending in 'l' or '-ment' American adds a second one where British does not – enroll (instead of enrol), instill (instil), fulfillment (fulfilment), installment (instalment);
3 in words like labour and colour American loses the 'u' – labor, color;
4 in words like centre and metre American reverses the last two letters – center, meter;
5 where British increasingly prefers '-ise' and '-isation' endings American keeps the 'z' – realize (realise), naturalization (naturalisation);
6 where British still uses 'ae' or 'oe' in words derived from Greek and Latin, American has the simpler 'e' form – etiology (aetiology), hemoglobin (haemoglobin), esophagus (oesophagus); in some common words like 'medieval' the 'e' form is now usual in Britain; 'foetus', which has the same etymology as 'effete', should logically be 'fetus' in Britain as in the US; this spelling is gradually catching on, particularly among doctors.

Here are American spellings for some common words (with the British in brackets):

ax (axe)
catalog (catalogue)

check, meaning bank bill of exchange (cheque)
cigaret (cigarette)
curb, meaning edge of pavement (kerb)
defense (defence)
disk, meaning any flat circular object (disc)
draft, meaning current of air (draught)
gray (grey)
inclose (enclose)
intrust (entrust)
offense (offence)
omelet (omelette)
pajamas (pyjamas)
pretense (pretence)
story, meaning floor in a building (storey)
tire, meaning rubber ring (tyre)

license is both noun and verb
practice is both noun and verb

It's noticeable that in several cases British spelling makes a distinction that is lost in American: curb, check, draft, story and tire are all common British words with their own separate meanings. British spelling also distinguishes between disk and program for the computer and the general words disc and programme – see below.

Program/programme

This confusing pair demands a separate entry. Most people assume that the Americans in their pursuit of simplicity took the English word 'programme' and shortened it. Not so: 'program' was the original English spelling. As HW Fowler wrote in his original *Dictionary of Modern English Usage* in 1926: 'It appears from the OED quotations that *-am* was the regular spelling until the 19th c., & the OED's judgement is: "The earlier *program* was retained by Scott, Carlyle, Hamilton, & others, & is preferable, as conforming to the usual English representation of Greek *gramma*, in *anagram, cryptogram, diagram, telegram &c."'

In other words there is no justification for 'programme'. It is a nineteenth-century French import that we could easily do without. But – as with so many examples of English spelling – it's difficult to see how we'll get rid of it.

Spelling of French words

French words have continued to flood into English since the Norman Conquest. Most of them are easily absorbed, so they become indistinguishable from English words, or they retain their separate identity, eg by being set in italic type. But a few imports cause problems in English because they are neither one thing nor the other: they seem to be stuck in mid-Channel, as it were. Should blond have an 'e' and if so, when? Can brunette be used of men or should it be brunet? What about confidant(e) and debutant(e)?

The French grammatical rule is that an adjective in the feminine form has an extra 'e', as in these examples:

blond(e), brunet(te), confidant(e), débutant(e)

Since in French an adjective agrees with its noun, a blonde woman ('a blonde') should logically have blond hair. But English doesn't really have 'gender' in the grammatical sense, so the decision comes down to style in the end.

'Chaperon(e)' is a curiosity. In French *chaperon* exists only as a masculine noun, but in English the (false) feminine form 'chaperone' has become far more common.

See also 'Accents' in the Punctuation chapter.

2
Grammar and style

The word 'grammar', which came into English from Greek (*gramma*, letter or written character) via Latin and Old French, has been used in all sorts of ways since the middle ages. For example, it gave its name to the schools founded in medieval and Tudor England specifically to teach the grammar of Latin. As Latin gradually gave way to English, the schools kept the name – and some still have it (whether or not they do much grammar teaching).

In the Jesuits' distinctive hierarchy of education the Grammar classes traditionally come sandwiched between Rudiments and Syntax, with Poetry and Rhetoric lording it above Syntax. So you might be in a Jesuit grammar school . . . in a Lower Grammar class . . . studying French or Latin grammar. And in a traditional classroom you might also have used a 'grammar' in the lesson – that is, a book containing the rules of grammar.

As a set of rules and conventions grammar is usually said to cover both the inflections, or changes, in words (love, loves, loved, loving), called morphology, and the way in which words are combined to form sentences, called syntax.

But just as the Jesuits have always seen syntax as separate from grammar rather than a part of it, some people want 'grammar' to cover the whole of English usage. So there are books with 'grammar' in the title that include such things as spelling, punctuation, figures of speech and literary devices.

After years in the wilderness grammar seems to be back in favour among modern linguists and educationists – but it's emphatically not 'traditional grammar'. To take an example cited by a linguistics professor (commenting on the introduction of 'modern' grammar), the subject should be 'relevant to all levels from the syntax of sentences through to the organisation of substantial texts' – which sounds rather like old-fashioned 'prose composition' (or in plain English 'essay-writing').

I prefer the straightforward, if limited, definition of grammar given in the third paragraph above, but I have added the word 'style' to the title of this chapter to make an important point. Style, in the context of this book, is the distinctive way in which somebody writes. To write well it's necessary to do more than avoid grammatical mistakes. Take the following example (which is certainly 'bad grammar'):

He's as old if not older than Fred.

It's bad grammar because it combines two expressions used to make a comparison ('as old as' and 'older than') but gives only one of them in full. Take 'if not older' away and you're left with 'He's as old than Fred' – which is clearly wrong. If the object of the grammar-correction exercise is simply to avoid error, the easiest thing to do is to put back the 'as' after 'old', adding a couple of commas:

He's as old as, if not older than, Fred.

But this is very stilted. Instead we could – I think should – write:

He's as old as Fred – if not older.

In the grammar examples that follow I try to make practical suggestions that do more than avoid error, though whether you follow my advice, of course, is up to you.

a, an: a is replaced by an before a vowel (an owl) unless the vowel is sounded as a consonant (a use), and before a silent 'h' (an hour). Some people in both speech and writing treat the 'h' in words like hotel, habitual, historic/al, horrendous and heroic as silent, using 'an' instead of 'a' – but this practice now seems very affected. It certainly isn't more correct than using a, so there's nothing wrong with:

He is staying at a hotel.

See also **article, the**

abbreviations and acronyms: abbreviations no longer need to be marked by full stops, whether they are truncations (where only the first part of the word is given, as in prof for professor or in for inch), contractions (where the first and last letters are given, as in St for saint or rd for road) or single letters (BBC, PD James).

Abbreviations that are spoken and written as words (Nato, Aids) are called acronyms and usually keep their initial capital. But some can be considered to have entered the language as ordinary words (awol for absent without leave, laser for light amplification by stimulated emission of radiation), losing the cap.

Since abbreviations should not be followed by words they include, expressions like 'an ITN news bulletin' and 'my pin (personal identification number) number' are technically incorrect and annoy some people. But they don't sound or look repetitive and it's difficult to object to them. *See also* the Punctuation chapter.

absolute adjective: an absolute adjective is one that can't logically be modified (eg strengthened or weakened by an adverb) because of its meaning. So something that is unique or impossible is just that: it can't be more or less unique or more or less impossible. But in everyday speech and writing this 'rule' is broken casually and often: rare events are 'almost unique'; hard tasks are 'virtually impossible'.

By contrast, the political novelist and journalist George Orwell breaks the rule in a carefully considered way. When the animals of Manor Farm overthrow their human masters and rename it 'Animal Farm' their key slogan is: *All animals are equal.* And when the pigs betray the revolution by seizing power, they replace this by the slogan: ALL ANIMALS ARE EQUAL BUT SOME ANIMALS ARE MORE EQUAL THAN OTHERS.

Which is obvious nonsense – but that is exactly what Orwell wants the reader to notice. He implies that perversion of language is a political matter: the grammatical rule he has the pigs break is part of logical thought and civilised behaviour. His practical advice to writers would be: don't break an important grammatical rule casually; break it by all means – but do it for a purpose.

absolute comparative/superlative: an adjective (good) can be used in the comparative (better) or superlative form (best) without an explicit comparison being made, eg 'The better-class hotels are intended for the best people.' This kind of language is particularly common in marketing and advertising.

absolute construction: in the following sentence the first part, in italic type, is an absolute construction:

The washing up finished, they went out.

The absolute construction has its own subject (the washing up) and is not joined to the sentence by a conjunction such as after. But the meaning is the same as in:

After they had finished the washing up, they went out.

absolute superlative: *see* **absolute comparative**

abstract noun: *see* **nouns**

accent marks, accents: *see* the Punctuation chapter.

accidence: *see* **grammar**

acronyms: *see* **abbreviations and acronyms**

active verb: *see* **verbs**

actually: *see* **rhetorical adverbs**

adjective phrase: an adjective phrase is based on an adjective and operates in the same way, qualifying or describing a noun or pronoun; the phrases below are in italics:

> That car is *faster than mine.*
> Mine is *far more comfortable.*

adjectives: an adjective qualifies or describes a noun or pronoun.

Demonstrative adjectives (this, that, these, those) identify a noun (this car, these potatoes). When used without a noun they become pronouns (this is my car).

Possessive adjectives (my, your, our, their) show ownership (my car).

Most other adjectives are *absolute adjectives* (final, perfect) or *adjectives of degree*. These can be:

- positive, used to describe something or somebody (the hot sun, a bad golfer);
- comparative, used to compare one thing/person with another (today's sun is hotter than yesterday's; this man is worse than that one);
- superlative, used to compare a thing/person with two or more other things/people (this is the hottest day of the year; this man is the worst of the three).

In everyday speech and writing people often use the superlative instead of the comparative to compare two things or people ('the best of the two alternatives'). Avoid this in formal writing.

See also **absolute adjective**

adverbial: an adverbial is a word, phrase or clause that functions like an adverb:

He ran *for about 10 kilometres.*
They're waiting *in the middle of the square.*
He set out *a month ago.*
She went to London *on business.*

adverb phrase: an adverb phrase is based on an adverb and operates in the same way:

He sees *very clearly.*
They got ready *as quickly as they could.*

adverbs: an adverb usually qualifies or describes a verb, adjective or other adverb:

He sees *clearly.* (adverb describes verb)
It was a *newly* minted coin. (adverb describes adjective)
He sees *very* clearly. (adverb describes adverb)

Adverbs used to link sentences are called *sentence adverbs* or *conjunctive adverbs* and are usually marked off by commas:

Life is expensive. Death, *however,* is cheap.

Note that 'however' can also be used as an ordinary adverb:

However good you are at punctuation you'll make the odd mistake.

- *There is no need for a hyphen after adverbs ending in -ly (see also the Punctuation chapter).*

agreement (concord): the principle of grammar that a singular subject must be followed by a singular verb and a plural subject by a plural one (number agreement); and that a pronoun must similarly agree with its antecedent (pronoun agreement).

See also **number agreement**

alliteration: alliteration is a figure of speech in which an initial sound is repeated in words that follow each other:

Sing a song of sixpence.

all right, alright: prefer all right to alright (which still looks wrong) unless you want your writing to look very colloquial.

always: *see* **rhetorical adverbs**

American usage: yesterday's 'Americanism' is today's standard British English – eg raise for bring up, or truck for lorry. Most of the linguistic traffic across the Atlantic and through the internet is one-way, so British variants like railway (for train) station will gradually become curiosities. *See also* the Spelling *and* Punctuation chapters.

amid/st: *see* **among/st**

among/st: the longer forms for among, amid and while (amongst, amidst and whilst) add nothing to the sense of these words. They say only that you prefer the long-winded and literary to the plain and concise. Even in its shorter form amid has a rather old-fashioned air, while amidst is archaic.

ampersand (&): the ampersand, which represents the word 'and', is used in company names such as Marks & Spencer; except in these cases it should be avoided in formal writing.

an: *see* **a, an**

and, but: there is no grammatical objection to the use of conjunctions such as 'and' and 'but' to start sentences. And there's no stylistic one, either. But to avoid a staccato effect in writing, don't overdo it.

See also **conjunction**

and which: *see* **that**

antecedent, the: a word or phrase which is followed by its pronoun. In the sentence 'He liked ice cream so much he ate it every day' *ice cream* is the antecedent of *it*.

antonym: an antonym is a word opposite in meaning to a word in the same language:

> start and stop

are antonyms.

any, anybody, anyone: as a pronoun 'any' can take either a singular or a plural verb:

> Has/have any of the players turned up yet?

As an adjective 'any' can also be singular or plural:

> Any player who wants a spare ticket can have one.
> Any players who want spare tickets can have them.

'Any' can also be used as adjective or pronoun to refer to uncount-able nouns like food:

> Will there be any food at the party? (adjective)
> Will there be any [food] at the party? (pronoun)

When 'any' is used as a singular adjective it is now usually followed by a plural pronoun:

> Any player who wants a ticket can have one sent to their home address.

It's the same with the singular pronouns 'anybody' and 'anyone':

> Anybody/anyone who wants a ticket can have one sent to their home address.

To object to this style, as some purists do, is silly. As Burchfield points out: 'Popular usage and historical precedent favour the use of a plural pronoun in such contexts.' To insist on the singular pronoun can lead to clumsy sentences like:

> Anyone who wants his or her ticket sent to his or her home address should remember to include it on his or her application.

apostrophes: there are three main uses of the apostrophe (which means 'a turning away' in Greek): the *possessive* apostrophe, such as 'the people's princess' (the princess of the people); in *contractions*, where something is omitted: 'I won't dance' for 'I will not dance'; to mark certain *plurals*, such as 'mind your p's and q's'. *See also* the Punctuation chapter.

apposition: two nouns or noun phrases placed next to each other referring to the same person or thing. In the sentence 'Samuel

Johnson, the lexicographer, was born in Lichfield' *Samuel Johnson* and *the lexicographer* are said to be 'in apposition'.

archaism: the use, conscious or unconscious, of a word or phrase that is out of date, with the effect (intended or not) of pomposity. A word like 'albeit' (for 'although, even if') is archaic; and so is the phrase 'suffice it to say' (for 'let it be enough to say').

article, the: the word 'the' is called the definite article; a/an is the indefinite article.

as . . . as: in comparisons 'as' needs to be followed by another 'as', not by 'than':

Children whose parents smoke are twice as likely to get bronchitis as [not than] those with non-smoking parents.

Expressions like 'as (good) as, if not (better) than' need to be handled carefully. There's an 'as' missing here:

Conditions here are as bad, if not worse than they were before.

Strictly speaking this should be 'as bad as, if not worse than', but this sounds stilted so turn the sentence round:

Conditions here as bad as they were before, if not worse.

assonance: assonance is a figure of speech where a vowel sound is repeated in words that follow each other:

The cat sat on my lap.

asterisks (*): asterisks are used to mark footnotes and to avoid printing swear words in full:

You stupid b***er!

See also the Punctuation chapter.

Australian usage: Australia uses British rather than American spelling, except in the case of the Australian Labor Party, but is even more vulnerable to Americanisation: potato crisps may still be so described on the packet – but everybody in Australia calls them 'potato chips'.

auxiliary verb: *see* verb

back-formation: forming a new word by shortening a longer one. Examples are: reminisce (from reminiscence), televise (from television), diagnose (from diagnosis) and legislate (from legislation). Usually the new word looks as though it is the original one. One reason why this is so is that the new, shorter word is almost always a verb. This process is a good example of the flexibility of English, though pedants object, eg to donate (from donation), enthuse (from enthusiasm) and liaise (from liaison).

barbecue: spell this word (from Haitian *barbacoa*) with a 'c' not a 'q'.

basically: not a word that says much; a padding word, basically.

basis: expressions like 'on a regular basis' and 'on a daily basis' are not an improvement on 'regularly' and 'every day'.

beg the question does not mean 'raise the question' although many people use the expression in this way. Technically, it means something more like 'avoid the question' – using as the basis of proof something that itself needs proving. It means arguing in a circle without a secure starting point. The assertion 'Falling house prices will create misery for everybody in Britain' begs the question of whether all British people own houses. If some of them don't, the statement is unlikely to be generally true.

bete noire: there is no need for a circumflex accent on 'bete' in English – but 'noire' needs its 'e' because 'bête' is feminine in French. If you want an English translation, it's bugbear.

between: there are two common mistakes made with between. It should be followed by 'and' not 'to' so the following is wrong:

> They always turn up between Wednesday to Friday.
> (between Wednesday and Friday)

And between should be followed by the objective case (him, me) not the subjective (he, I) so the following is wrong:

> This is strictly between you and I.
> (between you and me)

billion: the American billion (a thousand million) is now standard in Britain; in the past the British billion was a million million.

blob: *see* the Punctuation chapter

blond(e): in theory there's no problem: men are blond(s) and women are blonde(s) because in French an adjective takes 'e' in the feminine; whereas both men and women have blond hair because the word 'hair' is not feminine. But in practice the two words blond and blonde crop up all over the place used pretty indiscriminately.

The only sensible thing is to respect the theory. Then if you wrote 'Some gentlemen actually prefer blonds' (as an alternative to the movie title *Gentlemen Prefer Blondes*) you'd actually be saying something – about the sexual preferences of (male) gays.

bored (of): this 'mistake' is becoming the norm in colloquial English. People increasingly describe themselves as bored of (rather than with) anything from algebra to zoology. Opposing this change becomes pointless after a while – but it would still be smart to write bored 'with' rather than 'of' in a student essay or an article for publication.

both: this word should mean something. Adding it to a sentence like 'They were talking to each other' (so it becomes 'They were both talking to each other') is worse than pointless because the careful reader/listener is disconcerted and delayed by the redundant word.

See also **saying it twice**

brackets: *see* the Punctuation chapter

brunet(te): this is essentially an American, not a British, problem because in Britain the feminine form brunette is used only of women: neither brunet nor brunette is used of men. If both words are used, the rule that applies to blond(e) also applies to brunet(te): men are brunet(s) and women are brunette(s). But please let them all have brown not brunet(te) hair.

bullet point: *see* the Punctuation chapter

burglarize/burgle: burglarize is the American back-formation from 'burglary'; the British equivalent is burgle.

See also **back-formation**

burned/t: *see* **learned/t**

but: *see* **and**

café: keep the acute accent. *See also* the Punctuation chapter.

can, may: it's still possible to distinguish between can (being able to do something – being strong enough or skilful enough) and may (having permission to do it). But most people don't make the distinction by choosing between the two words. They tend to use can for both senses and ask 'Can I come?' or 'Can I help you?' rather than 'May I come?' or 'May I help you?'

An argument against the can/may distinction is that 'may' can mean possibility as well as permission. 'He may come' is more likely to mean 'It's possible that he will come' than 'He has permission to come'.

See also **may, might**

cannot, can't: *see* **contractions**

capital letters: *see* the Punctuation chapter

case: case is the name grammarians give to the differences in nouns, pronouns and adjectives according to the role they play in a sentence. Anglo-Saxon had a rich variety of case endings but modern English uses prepositions and word order instead. The traditional series of cases comes from Latin:

nominative **mensa** (table)
vocative **mensa** (O table!)
accusative **mensam** (table)
genitive **mensae** (of the table)
dative **mensae** (to or for the table)
ablative **mensa** (by, with or from the table)

In modern English the genitive (possessive) case of a noun is shown by the apostrophe (*see* the Punctuation chapter) plus 's':

the table's surface

Nouns show no other changes except to mark plurals (*see* the Spelling chapter) but pronouns have three different case endings: subjective, objective and possessive:

subjective	*objective*	*possessive*
I	me	mine
he	him	his
she	her	hers
we	us	ours
they	them	theirs
who	whom	whose
whoever	whomever	

category mistakes: this is Trask's term for mixing things up as in:

cold temperatures
a young age
cheap prices
fast speeds
The number of mistakes is remarkably few.
The probability of small wars has become more likely.

But it's the weather that's cold, not the temperature – temperatures are low. Similarly, a young person is someone of an early age; the price of cheap goods is low; if you run fast you travel at high speed. If there are remarkably few mistakes, their number is small. And a probability can't become more likely . . .

Avoid mixing the categories if you're trying to write carefully.

centre around, in, on: centre is followed by around (or round) more often than not – and it has been for more than a century, as Burchfield points out. But this use (or misuse) of a preposition differs from most of the others in that it defies logic: to centre *(a)round* something just isn't possible. Prefer revolve (a)round or centre in/on.

chaperon(e): although the French word *chaperon* is a masculine noun, English speakers have feminised it to 'chaperone'. So an older woman chaperones/acts as chaperone to a young one. The original form 'chaperon' is given in dictionaries but not often used.

clause: a clause is a group of words including a subject and a verb which forms part of a sentence. A compound sentence has two or more main clauses; a complex sentence has at least one main clause and at least one subordinate clause.

cliché: a cliché is a phrase, a sentence – but also a visual image, a response, a dramatic situation, nowadays almost any kind of expression – that was once vivid and striking but is now stale from overuse. The word cliché comes from the French *clicher* (to stereotype, ie make a plate for printing). As everybody knows (and the experts say at great length) you should avoid clichés. In fact, on the whole, not to put too fine a point upon it, when all's said and done, you should avoid clichés like the plague. But it's easier said than done . . .

clipped words/forms: these are words that started as short versions of longer words but are now words in their own right. They're not abbreviations, they count in Scrabble and they don't need apostrophes. Examples are:

bus for omnibus
fridge for refrigerator

mic/mike for microphone
ad/advert for advertisement
math (US)/maths (Britain) for mathematics
taxi/cab for taxi-cab (previously taximeter-cabriolet)

collective nouns: a collective noun refers to a group of individuals, such as government, council, committee, company, crew, family; it includes national teams, companies and other organisations. There is a clear difference here between British and American English. In the US a collective noun usually takes a singular verb; in Britain it takes a singular or plural verb according to sense:

The team is small [it has few players].

but

The team are small [the players are not big].
The cabinet is determined [it is seen as a single body].

but

The cabinet are discussing [it takes at least two to discuss].
The cabinet is divided [it must be seen as one before it can be divided].

but

The cabinet are agreed [it takes more than one to agree].

Whatever you do, don't mix the two forms close together. Don't write:

The cabinet is divided but they are discussing . . .

colon: *see* the Punctuation chapter

comma, comma splice: *see* the Punctuation chapter

common noun: *see* **noun**

comparative adjective: *see* **adjective**

compare like with like: be careful to compare like with like:

> Britain's weather sometimes feels worse than other countries.

is wrong because British weather is being compared with other countries – rather than with their weather.

compare to, with: use 'with' for routine comparisons – like with like or last year's results with this year's. Use 'to' when the comparison itself makes a point:

> Shall I compare thee to a summer's day?

complement: a verb that expresses not action but a state of being is inactive: it takes a complement:

> The man [subject] is [verb] ill [complement].
> He [subject] feels [verb] a fool [complement].

Some verbs can be either transitive (taking an object) or inactive:

> He feels the cloth [object].
> He feels ill [complement].

Whereas objects are in the objective case, complements are traditionally in the subjective case:

I see him [object].
It is I [complement].

But the common form 'It's me' is generally accepted and is certainly preferable to the stilted, formal-sounding 'It is I.'

complex sentence: *see* **sentence**

compound preposition: expressions like in connection with, in regard to and in relation to are wordy – avoid them if you can.

compound sentence: *see* **sentence**

compound words: *see* **hyphens** *in* the Punctuation chapter

comprise: comprise does not take 'of', and 'is comprised of' is just as bad:

The house comprises two living rooms and three bedrooms.

concord: *see* **agreement**

conditional tenses: there are two conditional tenses, the present and the past, both formed by adding would (I would think, I would have thought).

conjunction: conjunctions link:

1　two similar parts of speech – fit *and* well, slowly *but* surely
2　two sentences, whether they're separated by a full stop or not –

You may come. *Or* you may go.
You may come *or* you may go.

Whatever you may have been told there's no grammatical problem with 'and' or 'but' at the beginning of a sentence.

3   main clauses with subordinate clauses and phrases:

I will *if* you will.
I will go *as* a clown.

conjunctive adverb: *see* **adverbs**

contractions: contractions like can't for cannot and I'm for I am are increasingly common in ordinary writing. Take this book for example: if I want you to notice what I'm saying and understand it I will try to be as direct as I can. So sometimes I'll say I'll.

correlatives: correlatives are paired words that occur separately in a sentence such as:

as . . . as
both . . . and
not only . . . but also
neither . . . nor

See also **as . . . as**

courts-martial: this is the correct plural of court-martial; court-martials is wrong.

currently: an ugly way of saying now.

dangling modifier/participle (also unattached, floating): one of the most common grammatical mistakes, sometimes hilarious, always to be avoided. A modifying phrase should ideally be placed next to the part of the sentence it modifies; if it isn't, the reader is likely to be confused or at least irritated, as they will be by these examples:

> Literally a room for wine, the city is littered with these convivial boltholes.

> Born in Singapore, her Danish mother divorced her father.

> Having won the battle, the ground has shifted.

The city is not 'a room for wine'; her Danish mother was not born in Singapore; and the ground certainly didn't win the battle.

dash: *see* the Punctuation chapter

data, datum: data is, strictly speaking, a plural but the singular form, datum, sounds very stilted. It's advisable to use the plural form – followed by a plural verb – wherever possible:

> The data were inconclusive.

dates: *see* the Punctuation chapter

definitely: *see* **rhetorical adverbs**

deja vu: no accents are needed on 'deja'.

demonstrative pronouns: the demonstrative pronouns are this, that, these and those.

differ, different from, than, to: different from remains the recommended form in both British and American English. But the colloquial forms – to in Britain, than in the US – are increasingly common. As a verb, differ is always followed by from.

dos and don'ts: *see* the Punctuation chapter

dots: *see* the Punctuation chapter

double negative: one of the clear differences between standard English and non-standard or dialect forms concerns the double negative. In standard English a second negative negates the first – that is, it makes the statement positive:

> We can't not go to the party.

This means that not going to the party isn't an option: we have to go.

> It's not unusual . . . [as a rock singer, Tom Jones, once put it]

Whereas in non-standard English a second negative reinforces the first:

> I can't get no satisfaction . . . [according to another rock singer, Mick Jagger]

> I'm not going to no palace garden party . . . [as the punk rocker Johnny Rotten might have said if he'd been invited]

Because of the risk of confusion, be careful with the double negative – whichever way you use it.

double passive: be careful when one passive follows another:

> His advice was attempted to be followed.

Prefer: 'An attempt was made to follow his advice.'

double perfect: Trask quotes this example:

> I would have liked to have met Einstein.

It's a problem because 'have' is repeated: we need one 'have' or the other, not both. The first possible solution is:

> I would have liked to meet Einstein.

This means, Trask says, that I was alive at the same time as Einstein; that I might have managed to meet him; and that this would have given me pleasure – then. The second possible solution is:

> I would like to have met Einstein.

This means that I would be happy now if – somehow – I had managed to meet Einstein in the past. It doesn't imply that Einstein and I were alive at the same time.

dove: in Britain a dove is a bird; there are no signs of the American dove replacing dived as the past tense of dive – *but see* **sneaked, snuck.**

dreamed/t: *see* **learned/t**

driving, driver's licence: the American form 'driver's', as opposed to the British 'driving', is increasingly common in the UK.

due to: due is an adjective not an adverb so the following is technically incorrect:

> The use of hosepipes had been banned due to drought.

This is a quotation from one of JK Rowling's Harry Potter books cited by a critical reader to show the poor quality of her use of English. There are two lessons here. The first is that successful writers can make mistakes; the second that some readers care about them. If you want to avoid the 'due' mistake you can always use 'because of' instead. Nobody can object to that.

In fact there's a rule of thumb (quoted in the *Guardian* stylebook) that says when 'due to' means 'caused by' it's right, but when it means 'because of' it's wrong:

The train was late due to leaves on the line [because of – wrong].

The train's late arrival was due to leaves on the line [caused by – right].

dwarf, dwarfs, dwarves: the traditional British plural is 'dwarfs' and the 1937 Walt Disney film was *Snow White and the Seven Dwarfs*. On the other hand, Tolkien in his fantasies insisted on 'dwarves' and has had a huge influence. Although 'dwarves' may now be dominant in pulp fiction, 'dwarfs' is still preferable.

eg: eg means for example (it's short for the Latin *exempli gratia*); it does not need full stops; it should have a comma before it but not after it:

This book discusses various punctuation marks, eg the full stop.

either, neither: both these words refer emphatically to two possibilities: either go or stay; neither one thing nor the other. Either is followed by or, neither by nor.

As subjects either and neither are usually followed by a singular verb:

Either of these routes is possible.
Neither one thing nor the other pleases him.

But if both subjects are plural the verb is plural:

Either the French or the Italians have won.
Neither the French nor the Italians have won.

If there are two subjects and one is plural the verb agrees with the nearer one:

Either the captain or his players *have* arrived.
Either the players or their captain *has* arrived.

In speech and informal writing a plural verb is sometimes used even when both subjects are singular:

Have either John or Fred turned up yet?

But in formal writing it's better to stick to the singular.

elder, older: elder is the noun (the church elders), older the adjective (he is older than you); but elder is still used as an adjective in certain contexts, eg 'his elder brother', 'an elder statesman'.

ellipsis: *see* the Punctuation chapter

email: what started out as 'electronic mail', 'e-mail' for short, is increasingly 'email'.

émigré: émigré needs both its acute accents – the first is often forgotten.

epithet: a descriptive word or phrase applied to a person or thing to suggest an essential characteristic:

> Alfred *the Great* was the king who saved England from the Danes (and burnt the cakes).

> Saddam Hussein was given the epithet *Butcher of Baghdad.*

When the epithet is a noun or noun phrase it can be used without the person's name:

> *The Butcher of Baghdad* is dead.

See also **transferred epithet**

eponym, eponymous: an eponym is a person after whom something is named so 'the eponymous hero' of a book or play or poem is Robinson Crusoe or Hamlet or Samson – but the word 'eponymous' here is unnecessary: 'hero' would do.

equally as: 'equally as' is always wrong. 'She was equally as good as he was' mixes up two ways of saying the same thing. Instead write either:

> She was as good as he was.

or

> The two of them were equally good.

etc: etc means 'and the rest' (it's short for the Latin *et cetera*); it doesn't need a comma before it or a full stop after it.

etymological fallacy: the mistaken idea that the current meaning of a word must reflect its origin. The fact is that words often change their meanings in arbitrary ways.

exception that proves the rule: most uses of this expression are nonsense. The existence of an exception to a rule couldn't possibly show that the rule was valid. The expression can mean one of two things: either that an exception *tests* a rule (as in 'the proof of a pudding is in the eating') or that the making of an exception shows that there is a rule in the first place. 'Smoking permitted in this room' is evidence of a general ban on smoking.

fed up: like **bored,** fed up traditionally takes the preposition 'with' but 'of' is increasingly common:

> I am fed up of your complaints.

Stick to 'with' in formal writing but 'of' is here to stay.

feminine forms: feminine nouns ending in -ess are much less common than they were. In particular, Jewess and Negress are considered offensive and should not be used. A woman writer might be an author or a poet but never nowadays an authoress or a poetess. A woman teacher is no longer a schoolmistress; air hostesses and stewardesses have become flight attendants; women running things are managers not manageresses.

There is feminist pressure to extend this process to words like actress and waitress (women as well as men to be actors; waiter/waitress to be replaced by something like waitperson or waitron). But the terms actress and waitress are still current: they will offend few people and confuse nobody.

Some -ess words, eg lioness for the female lion and the titles baroness, countess and duchess, are not controversial.

few: few should only be used for what's countable:

> There were few people there.

Be careful of plural-sounding expressions which in fact measure quantity, extent, time etc:

> They were wearing few clothes.

sounds and looks wrong because 'clothes' is a noun only used in the plural. The sentence would be better as 'They were wearing very little.'

fewer, less: fewer for what's countable, less for quantity, so fewer trees but less wood. Thus at a supermarket checkout the fast lane should say 'fewer than 10 items' not 'less than 10 items' because what counts is the number of items not the weight or bulk of the goods or how much they cost. Above all, less should not be used of people. So sentences like this one are always wrong:

> There were never less than 30 or 40 people a day needing help.

But measurements of things like time, distance and money all take less not fewer:

> The journey takes less than two hours.
> The town is less than two miles away.
> I've got less than £2 on me.

figures: *see* the Punctuation chapter

figures of speech: a figure of speech is the use of words in a particular way to have a vivid effect. The more common ones such as **metaphor** and **simile** have separate entries.

finite and non-finite verbs: finite verbs have a subject (he walks); non-finite verbs are **infinitive** (to walk), **present participle** or **gerund** (walking), or **past participle** (walked).

first, firstly: there is no need for firstly (or secondly, thirdly and the others): first is both adjective and adverb:

> He was the first man there.
> To make an omelette, first break some eggs into a bowl.

floating participle: *see* **dangling modifier**

following: following is journalese meaning either 'after' or 'after and because of'

> Following the rain the sun came out.

Here there's no connection between the two events: it's after.

> The road is still closed following an accident.

Here the accident explains the road closure.

foreign words and phrases: don't litter your writing with foreign words and phrases. Don't use them to show off: use them only when you're sure that they express your meaning better than English words – and that the reader will understand them.

for you and I: *see* **prepositions**

four-letter words: there are more swear words in everyday writing than there used to be. But you don't have to be slavish. As with foreign words, use them only when you have to.

fragments: a fragment is an incomplete sentence. Subordinate clauses starting with conjunctions – although, because, since – shouldn't be cut off from their main clause by a full stop as in:

> We're going to have to educate people – provide classes outside school. Because the children aren't happy, nobody's happy with this.

Why separate the 'because' clause from the previous sentence? And what makes it worse is that the 'because' clause can be read as referring to 'nobody's happy with this' – after all, it's in the same sentence. Result: total confusion; reader has to reread (or maybe stop reading in irritation).

But there are cases where it does make sense to use a fragment – even one starting with something like because or since. Ask a rhetorical question, say – then give the answer:

> Why is everybody always picking on me? Because I can't sing in tune.

> How long has this been going on? Since Christmas.

In these examples the question mark makes the link between the complete sentence and the fragment. So the reader is prepared for what comes next.

from: from should be followed by to. So don't write:

> from 1939–45

but

> from 1939 to 1945 (or in 1939–45)

full stop: *see* the Punctuation chapter

future tenses: there are three basic future tenses:

> *simple:* I will see
> *continuing:* I will be seeing
> *completed:* I will have seen

There is also a fourth tense showing a mixture of continuing and completed action:

> I will have been seeing

See also **shall/will**

gender: there are at least three distinct meanings – or uses – of the word gender. The first is as a technical term in grammar where gender is applied to groups of nouns and pronouns labelled masculine, feminine and neuter. Nouns in English do not have gender though pronouns can be masculine (he), feminine (she) or neuter (it).

The second is as a trendy alternative to the traditional word sex, meaning the difference between male and female:

> a person of the female gender [instead of sex]

> The church is likely to remove from canon law all references to gender [ie to women as opposed to men].

And the third is a quite subtle idea introduced by feminists who wanted to contrast the biological differences between men and women (sex) and the social differences (gender); hence such phrases as gender identity and gender roles. As the language expert and feminist Deborah Cameron put it (in *Verbal Hygiene*, 1995), 'gender was a technical term which took its meaning from a contrast with sex'.

genitive: *see* **case**

gerund: a gerund is a verb-noun which has the same -ing form as the present participle:

> Seeing is believing.

Here both seeing and believing are gerunds.

The main problem with the gerund occurs when there's a noun or pronoun in front of it. People either write:

> I object to John smoking/I object to him smoking.

or they use a possessive:

> I object to John's smoking/I object to his smoking.

The non-possessive form is simpler, easier to use and increasingly accepted in formal writing. And with indefinite pronouns the non-possessive form is clearly dominant. Most good writers would avoid 'I don't object to anybody's smoking' and prefer:

> I don't object to anybody smoking.

get, got, gotten: get, for some reason, has traditionally been seen as a coarse little word not fit for polite society. Burchfield says he was made to rewrite sentences containing it as a schoolboy and the Longman guide advises against it in formal writing. But there really is nothing wrong with this powerful short word (though its effect is dulled by repetition).

Grammar and style

The past form of get in British English is always got – the American form gotten shows no sign of catching on, although we do have forgotten and ill-gotten.

grammar: grammar is the set of rules and conventions that are the basis of a language. Grammar is traditionally divided into two parts: morphology, the internal structure of words, dealing with inflections (or accidence); and syntax, the structure of phrases, clauses and sentences. Thus syntax forms part of grammar: you can't have 'grammar and syntax'.

In modern terms grammar is a branch of linguistics (the study of language), once called philology.

hanging participle: *see* **dangling modifier**

harass: harass has one 'r' unlike embarrass, which has two.

he or she, she/he, h/she etc: there's no need for any of this prissy nonsense if you're referring to both males and females in a general way:

If somebody comes, tell them to wait.

This is clear, idiomatic and considered correct by most people.

hiccup: this is the correct spelling; there's no argument at all for the curious variant 'hiccough' – which looks as if it means something else and should be pronounced 'hiccoff'.

homonym, homophone: both homonym and homophone refer to two or more similar words that are different in meaning. Homonyms are spelt (and usually pronounced) alike: bail (security) and bail (barrier) are homonyms. Homophones are pronounced alike but spelt differently: bail (security) and bale (evil) are homophones. In writing it's homophones that cause most of the trouble, as is shown by common confusions like complement/compliment, formally/formerly, hoard/horde, phase/faze, pore/pour.

See also the Spelling chapter.

hopefully: hopefully is a sentence adverb. There is no sound grammatical objection to using hopefully to mean 'it is hoped'. The main objection to it is that it's often vague:

> Hopefully he won't do it again.

shows that the speaker/writer thinks this but not who else thinks it.

See also **adverb**

house style: house style is the way a publication or printer decides to publish in matters of detail such as -ise/-ize spellings, single or double quote marks and when to use italics. Pointless variation is distracting: a consistent style helps the reader concentrate on what the writer is saying.

hove: hove comes from heave, which means lift or be lifted, retch, haul and also move (into position or sight), originally a nautical expression. In most senses the past tense of heave is heaved but in the nautical sense it's hove:

> The ship hove into view.

however: *see* the Punctuation chapter

hyperbole: hyperbole is a figure of speech consisting of extravagant and obvious exaggeration:

A million thanks!

hyphens: *see* the Punctuation chapter

I/me: in traditional grammar I is the subject, me the object:

I enjoy wine./Wine pleases me.

The same distinction applies to he/him, she/her, we/us and they/them:

He enjoys wine./Wine pleases him.
She enjoys wine./Wine pleases her.

See also **complement**

imperative mood: *see* **verbs**

imply, infer: *see* **mirror words**

inactive verbs: if a verb expresses not action but a state of being it's inactive and takes a complement.

See also **verb**

indefinite pronouns: the indefinite pronouns are, for example, anybody, none, each.

indicative tenses: there are three basic times (present, past, future) and three basic actions (simple, continuing, completed). So there are nine basic tenses.

See also **verb**

infinitive: the infinitive form of the verb usually, but not always, has 'to' in front of it. 'I want *to see*' and 'I can't *see*' are both examples of the infinitive.

intensive pronouns: intensive pronouns are, for example, myself, yourself, himself.

interjections: an interjection is a short exclamation added onto the main sentence. It either stands alone:

Alas! Woe is me!

Or it is linked to the sentence by a comma:

Hello, how are you?

interrogative pronouns: interrogative pronouns are, for example, who, whose and whom.

invariably: *see* **rhetorical adverbs**

irony: the use of words to express a meaning that is the opposite of what is said or written. Thus Robin Hood's sidekick was given the ironic name 'Little' John not because he was little but because he was big. This is the most common and straightforward form of irony.

Dramatic irony is the effect produced when the audience or reader of a play or epic poem knows more about its outcome than its characters do. An extension of dramatic irony is the condition in which a person seems mocked by fate or the facts, for example:

A woman survives a car crash and phones her husband to report her survival – only to be knocked down and killed a moment later.

Grammar and style

Socratic irony is the pretence of ignorance practised by the Greek
philosopher Socrates as a way of undermining an opponent's
argument.

italics: *see* the Punctuation chapter

jargon: the word is always derogatory, although qualifying it, eg as
medical jargon, reduces the gravity of the offence. Specialist termi-
nology becomes jargon when it's used in a general context.

journalese: journalese has been called the jargon of bad journalism.
Whether you're a journalist or not, you should avoid words like axe
(for sack), breakthrough, clampdown, jobless, slam and workshy . . .

kind, kinds: the noun 'kind' is singular so it should be:

> This kind of person . . .

'Kinds' is plural so it should be:

> These kinds of people . . .

knot: a knot is the speed of one nautical mile per hour, so a ship
travels at 10 knots. 'Knots per hour' is nonsense.

Latin words, phrases and abbreviations: in ordinary writing avoid
Latin wherever possible except to show your learning or make
facetious jokes. But a few Latin abbreviations are standard:

> *AD (*anno domini*), in the year of our lord (Jesus Christ), used for
> dates
> am (*ante meridiem*), before noon – in the morning
> eg (*exempli gratia*), for example

etc (*et cetera*), and the rest
ie (*id est*), that is
pm (*post meridiem*), after noon

Be careful with eg and ie, which are sometimes confused. Except in specialised contexts there is no need to use the other Latin abbreviations, such as:

cf (*confer*), which means compare
et al (*et alii/aliae/alia*), and the others (other men/women/things)
viz (*videlicet*), namely

lay, lie: in standard English (British and American) lay and lie are two separate words (though lay is the past tense of lie: 'I lay down'). Lay is a transitive verb with an object: you lay the table (present), laid the table (simple past), have laid the table (completed past). Lie is intransitive: you lie on the floor (present), lay on the floor (simple past), have lain on the floor (completed past).

Lie meaning 'to tell lies' is different again: you lie (present) becomes you lied (simple past) and you have lied (completed past).

Confusion between lay and lie is common.

leading question: a leading question is not hostile or unfair to the person it's directed to. It's a question that suggests an appropriate answer. A barrister who says to a witness 'You saw what happened, didn't you?' expects the answer yes. The barrister is leading the witness.

---

* Like BC (before Christ), AD is usually set in small capitals; BC comes after the date, AD before it:

Julius Caesar came to Britain in 55 BC.
St Augustine came to Britain in AD 597.

For non-Christians there are alternatives to BC and AD: BCE (before the common era) and CE (of the common era).

learned/t: with words like burn, dream, learn you can add either -ed or -t to make the past tense and past participle. But be consistent: 'I dreamt I burned the toast' is silly. One advantage of using -t for the past forms of learn as a verb is that you can distinguish them from the adjective learned (which means scholarly and is pronounced learnèd). Another is that -t is shorter than -ed.

least worst: this expression is very much in vogue – among other things it's used in a book title on medical ethics (*The Least Worst Death*) and it's a section heading in a book on how to think clearly ('least worst option' in *Thinking from A to Z*). The original idea has been traced back to a speech in 1947 by Winston Churchill, who told MPs: 'Democracy is the worst form of government except all the others that have been tried.'

In a sense least worst is a classic cliché – arresting at first, now hackneyed and increasingly corny, as in one of its 5 million (or so) Google hits: 'OK, anyone know which soda is least worst for you, Sprite or Coke?'

Particularly in formal writing prefer 'least bad' since 'least worst' doesn't, when you think about it, make sense.

less: *see* **fewer, less**

let alone: *see* **much less**

liaise: *see* **back-formation**

lie, lay: *see* **lay, lie**

like: this word has a variety of uses as well as the most obvious (we like chocolate):

1   to make a comparison:

Politicians, like footballers, sometimes have short careers./
Like footballers, politicians sometimes have short careers.

Points to note: commas are necessary to avoid confusion
with 2; it is essential to compare two things of the same
category so the following is wrong (see **dangling modifier**):

Like footballers, a politician's working life can be short.

2   to give an example:

Politicians like Tony Blair sometimes extend their careers
after retiring.

Point to note: commas should not be used here to avoid
confusion with 1.

3   as a trendy parenthetical filler:

He's, like, a typical politician.

Point to note: commas are necessary to avoid confusion with
'He's like a typical politician' (which would be a comparison
meaning 'he resembles a typical politician').

4   to mean something like 'so to say, as it were' at the end of
a sentence in various country dialects:

It's comfortable, like.

5   as a conjunction:

They didn't talk like other people talked.

Of these five uses of like only the first one (comparison) has universal approval in formal writing. But the second (example) is endorsed by The *Economist* as an alternative to 'such as' and is increasingly accepted. Keep the other three for informal writing.

likely: likely is an adjective meaning probable (it's likely to rain) and an adverb meaning probably. In the US the adverb is used by itself (in that case he'll likely take the bus) but in Britain it's necessary to qualify it in some way:

> quite likely, very likely, more likely, most likely, more than likely, as likely as not

could all be used here – but likely by itself is not yet generally acceptable.

literally: literally has a precise meaning: 'I am not using a metaphor.' In other words 'I mean exactly what I'm saying':

> He literally exploded with anger.

This means rather more than that he was very angry indeed. In fact it means that bits and pieces of him probably had to be recovered from the ceiling after the explosion.

People use 'literally' to hype up their prose whereas, logically, it can only be used to do the opposite. Sometimes they try to justify using the word by qualifying it – putting an 'almost' or a 'more or less' or a 'perhaps' in front of it. But this is nonsense:

> He almost literally exploded with anger.

Either he ended up on the ceiling or he didn't.

Because literally is so generally misused, millions of people now put 'quite' in front of it – to say 'I really mean it':

He quite literally exploded with anger.

But when you think about it this cliché means:

'He literally literally exploded with anger.'

And the matter doesn't end there since expressions like 'literally quite literally' and 'quite literally in fact' have been reported . . .

See also rhetorical adverbs

litotes: litotes is a figure of speech which is the opposite of hyperbole or exaggeration. It makes a positive assertion by understatement or even by saying the opposite. Examples are:

'Rome is no mean city' (instead of 'Rome is a great city').
'It was nothing' (said by the man-of-the-match).

-ly adverbs: -ly adverbs do not need hyphens. *See also* the Punctuation chapter.

major: major is one of those words used to inflate the importance of something; it usually means just 'big'.

majority: majority can only be used of countable things so you can't write:

The majority of the meal was inedible.

In theory you could write:

The majority of the courses were inedible.

But that's hardly an improvement on 'Most of the courses were inedible.' Phrases like 'the majority of cases [or courses]' are usually just padding.

In politics (and vote-counting in general) a majority means the greater number of votes. In a British election a candidate wins by a majority of X (the difference between their total and that of the candidate who comes second). A winner who gets more than half the votes has an absolute majority; a winner who doesn't has a relative majority. By contrast, in the US and Canada, only an absolute majority is called a majority; a relative majority is called a plurality.

malapropism: this is a ludicrous misuse of long words (from the character Mrs Malaprop in Sheridan's play *The Rivals*), such as 'a nice derangement of epitaphs' (for 'arrangement of epithets').

may, can: *see* **can, may**

may, might: there's a key distinction between these words. What confuses people is that in some contexts the distinction is one of degree whereas in others the two words mean totally different things.

I may come to the party./I might come to the party.

The difference here is one of degree: 'I might come' is more tentative than 'I may come.'

But with:

He may have come to the party.

we don't know whether he did or not. Whereas with:

He might have come to the party (if he'd known it was on).

we know he didn't come: the 'might' makes that clear.

Substitute 'may' for 'might' – as happens more and more in Britain – and the result is confusion. In:

He may have come to the party if he'd known it was on.

the two halves of the sentence don't match.

medium, media: media is the original Latin plural of the word medium. The other plural (used when we're talking about people who claim to be in touch with the spirits) is mediums. Although media is often used with a singular verb nowadays ('The media is responsible for dumbing down Britain'), this irritates careful readers – and nobody can possibly object to:

The media *are* responsible for dumbing down Britain.

The plural makes more sense.

meet: when meet means 'come face to face with' there's no need to add 'with' (still less 'up with'):

Fred met Joan at the station.

But use 'with' when meet means 'chance to experience':

He met with an accident.

metaphor: a metaphor is a figure of speech in which something is called by the name of what it resembles. Unlike a **simile,** which is introduced by like or as (he eats like a pig), a metaphor makes an explicit statement:

They are making pigs of themselves [eating greedily].

Ordinary English is full of words and phrases which are metaphorical in origin:

> She flew into a rage.
> He stormed out of the house.
> It was raining cats and dogs.

When these stock expressions stand out they are seen as **clichés**. Opinion is divided on clichés but nobody defends the mixed metaphor, in which two separate metaphors are used close together – to ludicrous effect:

> He has been made a sacrificial lamb for taking the lid off a can of worms.

metonymy: a figure of speech in which the name of a person or thing is replaced by the name of something related to it:

> He is a lover of the bottle [he likes drinking].

minority ethnic: the two words 'ethnic minority' (a minority consisting of people defined by their ethnicity) are sometimes transposed as in:

> the position of minority ethnic women

This is pointless and confusing.

mirror words: mirror words describe the same action or relationship from two opposite points of view: if I lend you something, you borrow it. But some people put it the wrong way round, substituting lend for borrow:

> Can I lend your book, please?

Other examples: teach/learn, infer/imply, ancestor/descendant.

mixed metaphor: *see* **metaphor**

Ms: women's forms of address remain a problem despite the introduction of Ms. This was intended to replace Miss and Mrs, which show a woman's marital status, and become the equivalent of Mr. But many British women don't call themselves Ms and would prefer not to be addressed as such. So when writing to or about a stranger it's probably safer to use no title at all, particularly since titles generally are used less and less.

much less, let alone: much less, let alone and similar expressions must follow a negative to make sense:

> I didn't see him, much less/let alone have a drink with him.

myself: myself has two accepted uses:

1   as an emphatic variation on I/me, tacked onto it:

> I myself couldn't understand it. I couldn't understand it myself.

2   as a reflexive:

> I try not to contradict myself.

Myself is also misused as a substitute for I/me, often because the writer seems to feel that I/me would be too direct:

> The director and myself will be there.
> Please inform the director and myself.

Use I in the first case, me in the second.

names: *see* **nouns**

negative: *see* **double negative**

neither: *see* **either, neither**

none: there's a strange superstition that none must be followed by a singular verb. Stranger still, the authorities on the use of English have been trying to correct it for decades. Here's HW Fowler in the first edition of *A Dictionary of Modern English Usage* (1926):

> none. 1. It is a mistake to suppose that the pronoun is sing. only & must at all costs be followed by sing. verbs &c.; the OED [*Oxford English Dictionary*] explicitly states that pl. construction is commoner.

So there can be no possible objection to sentences like:

> None of the guns were loaded.

As the Longman guide says:

> None may be followed by a singular or a plural verb as the sense requires.

non-finite verbs: *see* **verbs**

nouns: nouns are the names of people and things. They are either ordinary nouns called *common* (thing, chair) or special nouns called *proper* (George, Tuesday). Proper nouns often take a capital letter. *Abstract* common nouns refer to qualities (beauty, honesty), emotions (anger, pity) or states (friendship, childhood).

In general, nouns are singular (thing, man) or plural (things, men). But some nouns are the same in the singular and the plural (an aircraft/several aircraft, a sheep/a flock of sheep) and some are used only in the plural (scissors, trousers). Nouns that refer to collections of people and things (the cabinet, the team) are known as *collective* nouns.

number agreement: in general a singular subject takes a singular verb and a plural subject takes a plural verb. But some subjects are plural in form and essentially singular while others are singular in form and essentially plural.

An example is the word number itself. 'A number is stamped on each computer' is a straightforward singular; and so is 'The number of computers needed has gone up'. But 'a number of computers' – meaning many – takes the plural:

A number of computers are needed.

In the same way expressions like a crowd of people and a gaggle of geese are usually followed by plural verbs.

Per cent takes a singular verb when it refers to quantity (20 per cent of his time is spent gardening) but a plural one when it refers to number (20 per cent of those polled were in favour).

See also: **collective nouns, per cent**

numbers: *see* 'Numbers, fractions, dates' in the Punctuation chapter

object: *see* **verbs:** 'Transitive verbs and objects'

objective case: *see* **pronouns**

one and you: the choice between 'one' and 'you' to make general statements – 'one cannot complain'/'you can't complain' – is simple:

'one' is formal and distant, 'you' is colloquial and direct. The more informally you write, the more you'll use 'you'. What you mustn't do is mix up the two styles:

When you think about it, one should write carefully.

is just silly. But that doesn't stop people doing it.

only: according to the purists only should be placed next to the word or phrase it qualifies:

I'm here only for the beer.

But the pragmatists say only should be placed where it naturally falls:

I'm only here for the beer.

In ordinary writing – as in speech – the pragmatists have the better of the argument.

onomatopoeia: onomatopoeia is a figure of speech in which the sound of the words used helps to suggest the meaning:

He has a hacking cough.

onto/on to: onto should be one word – but only when it means 'to a position on':

The cat jumped onto the table.

Where 'on' and 'to' are quite separate words they should be kept apart:

After university he went on to write books.

opposite meanings: various words in English have opposite meanings:

> (to) cleave: divide (cleft stick) and stick firmly
> (to) dust: clean (remove dust) and sprinkle (eg sugar)
> fast: not moving (as in stuck fast) and rapid
> (to) head: remove the head/top and supply a head/top
> (to) let: allow and prevent (from which we get a let in tennis and the legal expression 'without let or hindrance')
> (to) overlook: look over and fail to see
> quite: fairly (quite good), very (quite excellent) and exactly (quite so)
> seeded: sown with seed and (of fruit) with the seeds removed

Oxford comma: *see* 'Comma' in the Punctuation chapter

oxymoron: a figure of speech which combines contradictory terms:

He is a cheerful pessimist.

paragraph break: *see* the Punctuation chapter

parentheses: *see* the Punctuation chapter

participles: there are two participles, the present (seeing) and the past (seen); they are used to make up the basic tenses of the verb (I am seeing, you are seen). The participles are also used as adjectives (a far-seeing statesman, an unseen passage) and in phrases (seeing him in the street, I stopped for a chat). The gerund has the same -ing form as the present participle but is a verb-noun.

parts of speech: traditionally, there are eight parts of speech – noun, pronoun, adjective, verb, adverb, preposition, conjunction and interjection, with the article (a/an or the) now often added to the list instead of being considered an adjective. There are various possible subdivisions: verbs can be 'auxiliary'; pronouns can be 'demonstrative' and 'possessive'. Numerals can be included as a separate category.

passive verbs: *see* **verbs**

past participle: *see* **participles**

past tenses: *see* **verbs**

per: except in stock phrases like miles per hour and miles per gallon, try not to use 'per' if the rest of the sentence is in English:

> She earns £40,000 a year [not per year].

per cent, percent: per cent (two words) is British; percent (one word) is American.

personal pronoun: *see* **pronouns**

phrase: a phrase is a group of words without a verb forming part of a sentence.

plurality: *see* **majority**

plurals: *see* the Spelling chapter

possessive: *see* **adjectives, pronouns**

prefix: *see* **hyphen** in the Punctuation chapter

prepositions: a preposition links its object with a preceding word or phrase:

It's a case *of* mumps.
We're going *to* Blackpool.

After a preposition a pronoun should be in the objective case:

of me
to you
for her
by him
with us
from them

The most common mistake in using prepositions is to use the subjective instead of the objective case – in order to sound posh or formal or polite:

to *we* British (it should be 'us')
for my husband and *I* (it should be 'me')

Here are some other prepositions to watch out for:

absent *from* (not 'of')
acquiesce *in* (not 'to')
affinity *between*, *with* (not 'to', 'for')
agree *on* (a point), *to* (a proposal), *with* (a person or opinion)
alien *from* (not 'to')
arise *from* (not 'out of')

bored: *see* **bored**
capacity *for* (not 'of')
centre *on/in* (not 'around')
compare: *see* **compare**
comprise: *see* **comprise**
consider: no preposition (don't use 'as')
correspond *with* (a person), *to* (a thing)
credit *with* (not 'for')
die *of* (not 'from')
differ *from* (in comparisons, not 'to' or 'than'), *with* (a person when disagreeing)
different: *see* **differ**
dissent *from* (not 'to')
distaste *for* (not 'of')
fed up: *see* **fed up**
glad *at* (a piece of news), *of* (possession)
impatient *for* (a thing), *with* (a person)
independent *of* (not 'from')
indifferent *to*
martyr *for* (a cause), *to* (a disease)
meet: *see* **meet**
oblivious *of/to* (not 'from')
part *from* (a person), *with* (a thing)
prefer *to* (not 'than' or 'rather than')
prevail *against* (a thing), *on* (a person)
prevent *from*
protest *at/against*
reconcile *to* (a thing), *with* (a person)
taste *of* (food), *for* (the arts and other things)

prepositions to end sentences: ending a sentence with a preposition could possibly be bad style but certainly not bad grammar. The silly idea (derived from Latin) that prepositions must never end English sentences should have been killed off by Winston Churchill's comment (on a civil servant's clumsy avoidance of a prepositional ending): 'This is the sort of English up with which I will not put.'

present participle: *see* **verbs**

present tense: *see* **verbs**

program(me): *see* the Spelling chapter

pronouns: pronouns stand for nouns and noun phrases. They are used to avoid repetition or for emphasis. They can be:

> *personal* (I/me, you, he/him)
> *possessive* (mine, yours, his)
> *reflexive/intensive* (myself, yourself, himself)
> *relative/interrogative* (who, whose, whom)
> *indefinite* (anybody, none, each)
> *demonstrative* (this, that, these, those)
> *reciprocal* (each other, one another)

The noun that a pronoun stands for is called its antecedent. Pronouns, unlike nouns, can change their form according to the role they play in a sentence: I becomes me; he becomes him. This role of a noun or pronoun is called *case*. In modern grammar the personal pronoun can be subjective (I) or objective (me); or it can be possessive (mine).

proper noun: *see* **nouns**

p's and q's: *see* 'Apostrophe' in the Punctuation chapter

pun: a play on words alike or nearly alike in sound but different in meaning:

> What is an ig? An Eskimo house without a loo.

question: *see* **beg the question, leading question**

question mark: *see* the Punctuation chapter

quite literally: *see* **literally**

quotation marks, quotes: *see* the Punctuation chapter

really: *see* **rhetorical adverbs**

redundancy: *see* **saying it twice**

reflexive/intensive pronouns: *see* **pronouns**

regularly: *see* **rhetorical adverbs**

relative/interrogative pronouns: *see* **pronouns**

repetition: a word, sound or phrase can be repeated intentionally for effect:

> O Romeo, Romeo! Wherefore art thou Romeo?

reported speech: the traditional way of reporting speech indirectly is to move most tenses one stage back. Thus the direct quote 'I support Spurs' becomes:

> He said he supported Spurs.

'I have always supported Spurs' becomes:

> He said he had always supported Spurs.

'I will always support Spurs' becomes:

> He said he would always support Spurs.

With the simple past there is usually no change. 'I supported Spurs until they sold Dimitar Berbatov' becomes:

> He said he supported Spurs until they sold Dimitar Berbatov.

You can put 'had' before 'supported' for clarity/emphasis:

> He said he had supported Spurs until they sold Dimitar Berbatov.

But the present tense is used more and more. 'I support Spurs' then becomes:

> He says he supports Spurs.

rhetoric is a general term for the art of using language to persuade or impress others. Note particularly the rhetorical question which puts an assertion in question format for greater impact:

> Did you ever hear such a thing?

rhetorical adverbs: modern English, particularly journalism and advertising, uses a lot of rhetorical adverbs, words intended to grab the reader's attention without having too much meaning. Examples are actually, always, definitely, invariably, literally, really, regularly, routinely, truly, uniquely, virtually. Adding a qualifying word like almost or quite can make them sound worse.

rhetorical question: *see* **rhetoric**

routinely: *see* **rhetorical adverbs**

saying it twice: various common expressions are pointlessly repetitive, eg:

> to share a common bond – if a bond is shared it is held in common
> to self-censor yourself – self is redundant
> the reason is due to – due to is redundant
> to restrict solely – cut solely

scare quotes: *see* the Punctuation chapter

screamer: *see* 'Exclamation mark' in the Punctuation chapter

second: *see* **first**

semicolon: *see* the Punctuation chapter

sentence: a sentence is a word or group of words expressing a complete thought and ending with a full stop (or equivalent pause). It has a subject, the person or thing being discussed, and a verb, expressing action or a state of being (and it may have other elements such as an object):

> *subject*   *verb*
> The man   sees.

Sometimes the subject is not stated but understood:

> The old man lay down. And died.

In the second sentence 'he' is understood.
A single word can be a sentence:

> 'Let's go out.' 'OK.'
> 'Do you want something?' 'No.'

A sentence with only one verb is a simple sentence:

> The man sees the sun.

A sentence with two or more main verbs is a compound sentence:

> The man sees the sun and he closes his eyes.

A sentence with one or more main verbs and one or more subsidiary verbs is a complex sentence:

> The man who sees the sun closes his eyes.

sentence adverb: *see* adverbs

serial comma: *see* 'Comma' in the Punctuation chapter

sex: *see* gender

shall/will: the standard form of the future tense is now 'will' not 'shall' in all cases:

> I /you/he/she/we/they will go fishing on Wednesday.

In the past it was considered correct to use 'shall' after 'I/we' for the plain future:

I/we shall be late.

On the other hand, 'will' was reserved for emphasis or determination:

I /we *will* catch this train even if we have to run to the station.

With he/she/you/they the position was reversed: 'will' was used for the plain future and 'shall' for emphasis. This usage would now be seen as literary/old-fashioned.

But 'shall' is still used after 'I/we' in questions that make some kind of offer or suggestion:

Shall I phone for a taxi?

Whereas straightforward questions that ask for information take 'will':

When will we get there, d'you think?

she/her: *see* **I/me**

should/would: the standard form of the conditional tense is would, not should:

I/you/he/she/we/they would go fishing if it were sunny.

Many people would now write 'was sunny' instead of 'were sunny'.

sic: sic is Latin for so. It appears in square brackets in quotations to emphasise that what looks like a mistake was made in the original – it hasn't been added by accident.

simile is a figure of speech in which something is said to be like something else:

> My love is like a red, red rose . . .

simple sentence: *see* **sentence**

singular noun: *see* **nouns**

singular pronoun: *see* **pronouns**

slash: *see* the Punctuation chapter

sneaked, snuck: snuck, the (popular) American past tense of sneak, is increasingly common in British English; but sneaked is still used.

split infinitive: 'to boldly go' is traditionally called a split infinitive: the infinitive (to go) is split by an adverb (boldly). This was declared to be a mistake by eighteenth-century grammarians by analogy with Latin (in which the infinitive is only one word, eg *errare*, to err). But modern grammarians say that the preposition 'to' isn't really part of the infinitive anyway, so it can't be split . . .

Others have pointed out that some words have their present form because an adverb has been added before a simple verb (to under-take, to over-throw) and that new expressions are formed in exactly the same way: to sexually harass; to verbally abuse. Whatever else it is, therefore, a 'split infinitive' is not now considered a gram-matical mistake.

But a problem remains, partly because many people think there is a problem. To avoid a split infinitive they will turn a simple sentence into a clumsy one:

> It is illegal deliberately to help someone to die.
> He began actively to dislike me.

94

The adverb should be put back where it belongs, if it's necessary. (You could argue that in these, and many other, cases the adverb doesn't add very much.)

Some people go to the other extreme and insist on splitting when there's no possible point:

> It is pettifogging to not use the word art to describe cave paintings . . .

What's wrong with 'not to use'? After all Hamlet didn't say 'To be or to not be.'

square brackets: *see* the Punctuation chapter

subject: *see* **sentence**

subjective case: *see* **pronouns**

subjunctive mood: *see* **verbs**

subordinate clause: *see* **clause**

such as, like: *see* **like**

suffice it to say: this is an archaic expression with a verb in the subjunctive mood ('suffice it' instead of 'it suffices') meaning 'let it be enough to say' or 'I won't bore you with the details':

> Suffice it to say that war broke out on his birthday.

It's pointless to use this phrase unless you *want* to sound pedantic and old-fashioned – but if you do use it, don't make things worse by leaving out the 'it' (as some people do). 'Suffice to say' is just nonsense.

superlative: *see* **adjectives**

synecdoche is a figure of speech in which the part is used for the whole or the whole for the part:

All hands on deck!

synonym: a synonym is a word with the same (or nearly the same) meaning as another one in the same language:

start, begin and commence

are synonyms.

syntax: *see* **grammar**

tenses: *see* **verbs**

thankfully is a sentence adverb: *see* **adverbs**

that, which: there is a continuing problem with 'that' and 'which'. According to traditional grammar 'that' should be used in defining/restrictive/essential clauses:

This is the house that Jack built.

Whereas 'which' should be used in non-defining clauses:

They bought Fred's house, which was built in 1937.

'That Jack built' defines the house and doesn't have a comma before it; 'which was built in 1937' adds incidental information and should have a comma.

In the US the that/which distinction still rules formal writing; but in Britain it has long since ceased to do so. Many literate people – academics, novelists, journalists – don't always use 'that' for defining clauses. And the Queen (patron of the Queen's English) certainly doesn't.

transferred epithet: a curious feature of English in which an adjective is understood to modify something different from the noun that follows it:

> They were having a quiet cigarette.

tells you nothing about the cigarette (or cigarettes) they were smoking. Instead it tells you how they were smoking – ie quietly.

transitive verb: *see* verbs

truly: *see* rhetorical adverbs

uniquely: *see* rhetorical adverbs

variation: variation is using a different word or phrase to describe something so as to avoid repetition and make writing sound more impressive:

> Instead of talking about a *spade* I'll now refer to a *horticultural implement.*

The phrase 'elegant variation' was coined by Fowler in 1926. His essay quoted a reference by Thackeray to 'careering during the season from one great dinner of twenty *covers* to another of eighteen *guests* . . .'

The spirit of Thackeray lives on in every football reporter who follows a reference to the footballer Robbie Keane by a series of descriptive phrases to avoid repeating his name – the Liverpool striker, the Republic of Ireland international, the ex-Tottenham star . . .

verb-noun: *see* gerund

verbs: verbs express action or a state of being or becoming. They can be finite because they have a subject (he thinks) or non-finite because they don't (to think). The tense of a verb shows whether it refers to the past, the present or the future. Tenses are formed either by inflecting the verb (changing its form: he thought) or by adding an auxiliary verb (he will think) or both (he has thought). Verbs can be active (he thinks) or passive (it was thought).

Finite verbs can be:

> indicative, either statement (he thinks) or question (does he think?)
> conditional (I would think)
> subjunctive (if he were to think)
> imperative (go on, think!)

Non-finite verbs can be:

> infinitive (think, to think)
> the present participle or gerund (thinking)
> the past participle (thought)

Indicative tenses
There are three basic times (present, past, future) and three basic actions (simple, continuing, completed). So there are nine basic tenses:

	SIMPLE	CONTINUING	COMPLETED
Present	I think	I am thinking	I have thought
Past	I thought	I was thinking	I had thought
Future	I will think	I will be thinking	I will have thought

Three other tenses show a mixture of continuing and completed action:

Present: I have been thinking
Past: I had been thinking
Future: I will have been thinking

Traditional grammar distinguished between the first person singular (I), the second person singular (thou), the third person singular (he/she), the first person plural (we), the second person plural (you) and the third person plural (they). But modern English has dispensed with the second person singular (thou is archaic), and in most verbs only the third person singular differs from the standard form:

I think
You think (singular)
He/she thinks
We think
You think (plural)
They think

Conditional tenses
There are two conditional tenses, the present and the past, both formed by the addition of would:

I would think
I would have thought

Subjunctive tenses
The verb forms for the subjunctive mood are much the same as for
the indicative – which is one of the reasons for confusion between
the two. But there are two exceptions. The third person singular,
present tense, changes as follows:

INDICATIVE
'She *has* faith' becomes
'He *finds*' becomes

SUBJUNCTIVE
'If she *have* faith'
'Should he *find*'

The verb 'to be' changes as follows:

Present

INDICATIVE
I am
He/she is
We are
You are
They are

SUBJUNCTIVE
I be
He/she be
We be
You be
They be

Past

INDICATIVE
I was
He/she was

SUBJUNCTIVE
I were
He/she were

'We were', 'you were' and 'they were' remain unchanged.

Transitive verbs and objects
A finite verb may have an object, the person or thing that receives
the action of the verb. This kind of verb is called transitive:

SUBJECT | VERB | OBJECT
The man | sees | the sun.

An object may be direct or indirect:

SUBJECT	VERB	DIRECT OBJECT	INDIRECT OBJECT
The man	gives	the dog	to his son.

SUBJECT	VERB	INDIRECT OBJECT	DIRECT OBJECT
The man	gives	the dog	a bone.

Intransitive verbs
If nothing receives the action of the verb it's called intransitive:

SUBJECT	VERB
The man	walks.

Intransitive verbs are often followed by something to extend their meaning but this is not called an object:

The man walks slowly [adverb].
The man walks to work [adverbial].

Active and passive verbs
A transitive verb is in the active voice. It can also be turned round so that it's in the passive voice:

ACTIVE	PASSIVE
The man sees the sun.	The sun is seen by the man.

Be careful when you combine the passive with a participle:

The workers were penalised by sending them back.

is incorrect because the subject of the main verb (the workers) is different from the (implied) subject of the participle whereas in a sentence like this it must be the same:

The workers were penalised by being sent back.

is correct – and so is:

They penalised the workers by sending them back.

Inactive verbs and complements
If a verb expresses not action but a state of being it is inactive and takes a complement:

SUBJECT	VERB	COMPLEMENT
The man	is	ill.
He	feels	a fool.

Some verbs can be either transitive or inactive:

He feels ill [complement].
He feels the cloth [object].

Agreement of the verb
The verb must agree with its subject in person and number:

I give.

but

He gives [person].

Spelling is important.

but

Spelling and grammar are important [number].

virtually: *see* **rhetorical adverbs**

vogue words: there are so many that a list would be otiose (super-fluous). The letter I, for example, gives us:

> *iconic*: adjective used to describe anything vaguely memorable or well-known
>
> *impact*: verb meaning to have an effect (on)
>
> *inchoate*: adjective which technically means just beginning or undeveloped but is also used to mean chaotic, incoherent or disorderly
>
> *indicate*: verb used to mean point out, show, imply, suggest, state etc
>
> *inform*: verb used to mean shape or inspire (as opposed to its ordinary meaning of tell)
>
> *ironic*: adjective used to mean strange, coincidental, paradoxical, amusing . . .
>
> *issues*: plural noun used to mean problems

waitress: *see* **feminine forms**

we/us: *see* **I/me**

web, website: no caps, 'website' one word

what: 'what' can be a problem at the beginning of a sentence. The experts disagree about which of these is correct:

> What I like *is* holidays abroad./What I like *are* holidays abroad.

Or to put it another way, both forms are thought to be incorrect by some people. Instead try:

What I like is *a holiday* abroad.

whence: 'whence' is literary for 'from what place' so 'from' is not necessary.

wherefore: wherefore is an archaic way of saying why (not where).

which: *see* **that**

while/whilst: *see* **among/st**

who, whom: in traditional grammar 'who' is subjective:

Who is your guest?/Who are you?

and 'whom' is objective:

Whom did you invite?/To whom did you send an invitation?

But in speech and increasingly in writing 'who' is replacing 'whom':

Who did you invite?/Who did you send an invitation to?

'Whom' still crops up in the stock phrase 'to whom it may concern' but not often elsewhere. It can be used by mistake:

The woman, whom he knew was a teacher, gave him a book.

Here 'whom' should be 'who' because it is subjective – he knew that *she* (not 'her') was a teacher.

whoever, whomever, whomsoever: if 'whom' is dying, 'whomever' and 'whomsoever' are dead.

will/shall: *see* **shall/will**

with: just as the preposition 'with' doesn't affect the verb in:

> Spelling, with grammar, is important.

so it doesn't affect the subject in:

> With her husband she faced the future.

world wide web: three words, no caps.

would/should: *see* **shall/will**

Xmas: some people object to this common short form for Christmas on the grounds that it's vulgar, commercial etc. In fact the X represents the first letter (*chi*) of the Greek word for Christ.

year's/years' time: there's no need for the word 'time' after expressions like 'in a year' and 'in two years'.

you and I (for): *see* **prepositions**

you and one: *see* **one and you**

3
Problem words

There are all sorts of reasons why English has so many words that cause problems – to native speakers and foreigners alike. The first point to notice is the sheer volume and variety of its vocabulary. For example, there may be several English words meaning the same thing: start, begin, commence – which one best fits the context? Or there may be several similar-sounding words meaning different things: assure, ensure, insure – which one says exactly what you want to say?

English is full of confusing pairs like **abrogate** and **arrogate**, **forceful** and **forcible**, **systematic** and **systemic**. It has pairs of words with **opposite meanings**: let, cleave, overlook. Some words have (at least) two related but different meanings: **aggravate, contemporary, decimate**. Then there are **mirror words**, which describe the same action or relationship from two opposite points of view, eg lend and borrow.

Homonyms and **homophones** both refer to two or more similar words that are different in meaning. Homonyms are spelt and usually pronounced alike; homophones are pronounced alike but spelt differently. There are numerous examples of homophones in this chapter and others are included in the Spelling chapter.

Then there are **vogue words** like iconic and ironic, which suddenly become fashionable; they seem to mean less and less as they crop up more and more. And there's a general tendency to use words that are formal, pompous or pretentious instead of good clear English. Words like this – **eschew** and **quaff**, for example – are labelled 'literary' here to suggest that they strike a false note.

There's a particular problem with foreign words in English, whether they come from ancient Greek or Latin or modern languages. Phrases like **hoi polloi** and words like **decimate** cause difficulty because some people want to use them precisely – otherwise what's the point? – whereas others can't be bothered. The same goes for words imported from modern languages. As **embonpoint** crossed the Channel it lost its original French meaning (plumpness) and acquired a trendy British one (cleavage); as **entrée** crossed the Atlantic, it ceased to mean the first course in a meal and became main course.

The examples that follow illustrate some of the problems to be found in a selection of English words. Use them with care. Sometimes the best advice might be not to use a particular word on the grounds that, even if you're using it carefully, your reader may not get the message.

abrogate, arrogate: abrogate is cancel, revoke; arrogate is claim for yourself.

accolade, acolyte: an accolade is high public praise; an acolyte is a faithful follower.

accrue: come as a natural growth or increment (interest accrues on money invested), is now often turned into an active verb meaning acquire or accumulate ('Schools at the bottom of the heap accrue more of society's downtrodden', according to a professor of education).

acute, chronic: acute is sharp or severe; chronic is lingering or lasting. This distinction, common in medicine, is also made in other fields. But chronic is popularly used to mean very bad (City's marking was chronic).

adapter, adaptor: an adapter is someone who adapts something, eg a novel for the stage, while an adaptor is what you need when your electric plug doesn't match the socket.

address: address as a verb has several straightforward uses (you address a meeting, an envelope, a golf ball), but it's also political and management jargon for face, apply yourself to, answer (a plan to address the problem).

adherence, adhesion: both words come from adhere which means stick (to), in the literal sense, and keep (to). Adhesion and its adjective adhesive refer to sticking (eg glue); adherence and adherent refer to keeping, belonging (eg to a principle or organisation).

admission, admittance: both words come from admit but they are used differently. Admission is used of something admitted or conceded (admission of guilt) and the price of entry (admission £5), while admittance is particularly used of attempts to keep people out (no admittance).

adverse, averse: adverse is opposed, unfavourable; averse is disinclined, reluctant.

affect, effect: (to) affect, meaning put on, pretend to have (he affected a false superiority), and (to) affect, meaning influence, have an effect on (the weather affected ice-cream sales), are words of different origin although they are written and pronounced in the same way. They can be confused with (to) effect, which means to carry out or accomplish (he effected the sale). As a noun affect (in psychology an emotional state) is rare while effect is common. It means the result of an action (the effect of the weather was increased sales) and in the plural, goods or property (his personal effects).

aggravate is used to mean make worse (when he fell down he aggravated the injury) and also annoy (he had aggravating views on the economy). Some people object to the second use.

akimbo has a precise meaning: with hand on hip and elbow out. So legs that are apart can't be akimbo and nor can arms that are waving about.

albeit is a formal, archaic-sounding alternative to although, even if (his voice, albeit the accent was foreign, was musical).

alibi: alibi is elsewhere (when a crime is committed) and is a weak alternative to excuse for failure in general.

allusive, elusive: allusive is alluding, hinting; elusive is difficult to find, deceptive.

amend, emend: amend is improve; emend is remove errors in a text.

anticipate is used by careful writers to mean forestall or act in advance or come before (on social spending opinion moved to the right in the 1970s anticipating Thatcher's victory) and by pompous writers to mean expect (we don't anticipate rain).

appraise, apprise: appraise is assess the value of; apprise is inform, give notice to.

arguably is often used instead of possibly/probably. Since these words are more precise it's probably better to choose one or the other rather than blur the issue by using arguably.

arrogate: *see* **abrogate**

assist, assistance: formal alternatives to help.

assure, ensure, insure: assure is give confidence to; ensure is make sure that something happens; insure is arrange insurance.

auger, augur: an auger is a tool for boring holes; an augur was an ancient Roman soothsayer, so to augur well/badly is to be an encouraging/discouraging sign.

autarchy, autarky: autarchy is absolute power; autarky is self-sufficiency.

aver: aver is a literary alternative to say.

averse: *see* **adverse**

balmy, barmy: balmy, from balm (ointment), is fragrant, soothing, while barmy, from barm (fermenting liquor), is crazy (eg the Barmy Army, England's raucous cricket fans).

barbaric, barbarous: barbaric is primitive, uncivilised, but with no derogatory implication; barbarous suggests cruel or harsh.

base, bass: base is foundation and, as an adjective, low, humble, worthless, whereas bass (pronounced in the same way with a long a sound) is the lowest part in music. Bass with a short a is a fish.

bath, bathe: you bath a baby (but take or have a bath yourself), bathe a wound and bathe in the sea.

bathos, pathos: bathos is anticlimax, a ludicrous fall from the elevated to the ordinary (after a grand and formal opening the play descended into bathos); pathos is the quality that excites pity or sadness (the play's pathos comes from the hero's inability to understand himself).

biannual, biennial: many people are confused about which one of these means twice a year and which one means every two years, so it's safer to spell out what you mean instead (biannual is twice a year, biennial every two years).

billion: the American billion (a thousand million) has replaced the old-style British one (a million million).

blanch, bleach, blench: they all mean to make or become white but almonds are blanched, clothes are bleached and you blench from fear.

bogey, bogie, bogy: three different words. A bogey (named after the mythical Colonel Bogey) is a score of one over par at golf; a bogie is a trolley or child's racing cart; a bogy is a goblin or a piece of nasal mucus.

borrow, lend: *see* **mirror words** in the Grammar and style chapter

caddie, caddy: a caddie carries golf clubs; tea is kept in a caddy.

calendar, calender: a calendar tells you what day it is; a calender is a rolling machine for paper or cloth.

callous, callus: callous is cruel; a callus is hard skin.

canvas, canvass: canvas is cloth, whether for sails, tents or paintings; to canvass is to solicit votes.

carat, caret: a carat is a unit of measurement for gold and gems; a caret is an insertion mark in proofreading.

careen, career: to careen is to turn something (eg a ship) on its side for cleaning or repair; it's confused with the verb to career (rush headlong). But career as a noun (progress through life or in a particular activity) doesn't imply rushing.

celibate, chaste: to be celibate, for most people, is to abstain from having sex. But the original meaning of the word, 'unmarried' (from the Latin *caelebs*, single), has not disappeared completely. Catholic priests, for example, must remain 'celibate' – that is, they are not allowed to marry. At the same time they are not supposed to have sex: they must remain 'chaste'.

censer, censor, censure: a censer is a pan in which incense is burnt in a religious ceremony; a censor vets and can suppress published material; censure is blame.

chafe, chaff: chafe (irritate) is confused with chaff (tease).

chaste: *see* **celibate**

chauvinist: once an extreme nationalist (from the fictional character Nicolas Chauvin, one of Napoleon's veterans), now a sexist (originally 'male chauvinist pig').

chronic: *see* **acute**

classic, classical: the classics are Greek and Latin language and literature; classical refers to Greek and Roman culture and is the opposite of romantic; classic is used of anything outstanding, definitive or stylish including the five chief races in the English flat-racing season.

climactic, climatic, climacteric: climactic refers to a climax; climatic to the weather; climacteric to a critical period in human life.

cohort: originally, cohort (from Latin) meant a company of soldiers; by extension it became any group of people with something (eg age) in common; it's also (confusingly) used of an individual companion or follower. It even crops up when 'partner' would be the straightforward word, possibly confused with **consort** (Cherie Blair and her prime ministerial cohort).

coin: to coin is to invent, so saying 'to coin a phrase' before something very familiar has to be an ironical apology for a cliché; without the irony it's nonsense.

complacent, complaisant, compliant: complacent is smug, self-satisfied; complaisant is obliging, ready to condone; compliant is yielding, co-operative.

comprehensible, comprehensive: comprehensible is understand-able; comprehensive is inclusive.

comprise, consist of: as a formal alternative to consist of, comprise appears in ads by estate agents, who often mix the two expressions. That is, they add a redundant 'of' to 'comprise' (the accommodation comprises of/is comprised of four rooms). The correct formal expression is: 'The accommodation comprises four rooms.' But there is nothing wrong with 'consist of'.

compulsive, compulsory: compulsive behaviour, eg lying, results from an inner compulsion; compulsory means imposed by someone else.

concert, consort: from concert, musical performance, comes agree-ment or harmony (acting in concert); a consort is a companion or partner.

congenital, genetic: genetic or hereditary conditions are inherited; congenital ones date from birth without necessarily being inherited.

consensus: consensus doesn't need 'general' before it or 'of opinion' after it. If most people agree on something, the consensus is that . . .

consist of: *see* **comprise**

consort: *see* **cohort, concert**

contemporary: contemporary is used to mean both belonging to the same time (he was one of Dr Johnson's contemporaries) and modern, present-day (contemporary views of language).

contemptible, contemptuous: contemptible means despicable; contemptuous means scornful.

continual, continuous: if it rains continually it rains a lot but sometimes stops; if it rains continuously it goes on raining all the time.

co-respondent, correspondent: a co-respondent (with or without a hyphen) features in divorce cases; a correspondent writes letters or newspaper articles.

corps, corpse, corpus: a corps is an organised group of people, particularly in the army; a corpse is a dead body; a corpus is a collection of, eg, writings.

coruscate, excoriate: coruscate, sparkle, is confused with excoriate, strip the skin from, criticise severely.

coup, coupe, coupé: a coup is a blow or strike; a coupe is a shallow dish (and the dessert inside it); a coupé is a two-door car with a sloping roof; in the US the coupé loses its accent.

cow, cower, kowtow: to cow is to subdue, keep under; to cower is to crouch or cringe in fear; to kowtow is to grovel, abase yourself.

credible, credulous, creditable: credible is believable; credulous is easily taken in; creditable is trustworthy or praiseworthy.

crescendo: a crescendo is the rising of a sound towards a climax rather than the climax itself, so you can't 'rise to a crescendo'.

crevasse, crevice: a crevasse is an opening in a glacier or river bank; a crevice is a narrow crack in rock.

deadly, deathly: deadly is fatal, causing death (deadly poison); deathly is a poetical word meaning deathlike, pale (deathly face).

decimate: decimate has the traditional meaning of kill one man in 10 but since it is so often used to mean massacre or destroy, it's much safer to be explicit: say 'kill one man in 10' or 'destroy'.

decry, descry: decry is belittle; descry is literary for catch sight of.

deduce, deduct: deduce is infer by reasoning; deduct is subtract.

defective, deficient: defective is faulty; deficient is lacking in something.

definite, definitive: definite is precise; definitive is final and conclusive.

defuse, diffuse: to defuse is to make (eg a bomb) harmless; to diffuse is to spread, hence the adjective diffuse (widely spread, wordy).

delusion, illusion: delusion is false belief or hallucination (delusions of grandeur); illusion is false impression (optical illusion).

demise: demise is a legal or literary word for death.

dent, dint: two spellings of the same word meaning the hollow caused by a blow; 'by dint of' is literary for 'by means of'.

deprecate, depreciate: deprecate is deplore, protest against (he deprecated their behaviour); depreciate means both disparage and fall in value (his investment depreciated).

derisive, derisory: derisive is mocking (derisive laughter); derisory is laughable (a derisory amount).

detract, distract: detract is take away; distract is divert the attention of.

diffuse: *see* **defuse**

dilemma: a dilemma is more than an awkward problem. Strictly speaking it's a choice between two alternatives each of which is undesirable (the classic career woman's dilemma: whether to sacrifice time at work or time with the family).

dinghy, dingy: a dinghy is a small rowing-boat; dingy is dark-coloured or dirty.

dint: *see* **dent**

disassemble, dissemble: disassemble is take to pieces; dissemble is disguise, deceive.

discomfit, discomfort: discomfit is an old word meaning defeat, now often used (as though it were discomfort) to mean make uncomfortable (the bowler discomfited the batsman).

disinterest, disinterested: disinterest has the traditional meaning of impartiality but is now often used to mean lack of interest; disinterested (impartial) is similarly confused with uninterested. Most uses of disinterested now risk confusion.

distract: *see* **detract**

distrait, distraught: distrait is absent-minded; distraught is upset.

divers, diverse: divers is archaic for several; diverse is varied.

draft, draught: draft is used for selection (eg in conscription), a bank order and a preliminary sketch or written version; draught for something drawn, pulled or drunk, a current of air and the depth to which a ship sinks in the water.

drier, dryer: drier is the comparative of the adjective dry; a dryer is for hair.

dual, duel: dual is consisting of two (dual carriageway); a duel is a prearranged fight between two people.

economic, economical: economic is to do with economics or business or likely to be profitable; economical is thrifty or cheap.

effect: *see* **affect**

egoism, egotism: egoism is a philosophical theory; egotism is selfishness, hence egotistical.

egregious: egregious always means outstanding, exceptional, either good or bad. In Britain it's almost always a rather literary way of abusing or belittling somebody or something rather than praising them.

eke out: eke out has the traditional meaning of make (something) go further (he eked out his supplies by picking wild fruit) but is now often used to mean achieve with difficulty (by sheer determination they eked out a victory).

elderly: elderly has the traditional meaning of quite old but its most common use now is as a euphemism: 'the elderly', like 'senior citizens', is a polite (or patronising) way of saying 'old people'.

elegy, eulogy: an elegy is a mournful poem; a eulogy is a tribute to someone alive or dead.

elemental, elementary: elemental is connected with the elements; elementary is simple or rudimentary.

elicit, illicit: to elicit is to draw out; illicit is an adjective meaning illegal.

elusive: *see* **allusive**

embonpoint: embonpoint is a French word meaning plumpness in general. In Britain, for some reason, it is now a euphemism for a woman's breasts (he leered at her embonpoint).

emend: *see* **amend**

enhance: to enhance is to improve; it's a positive word that doesn't mean make worse (so 'enhance the injury' is wrong).

enormity, enormous, enormousness: enormous can mean immense (he went to enormous trouble – no criticism implied) or excessive (he has an enormous head – he'd probably prefer a smaller one). Enormousness (great size) is a clumsy word, often replaced by enormity – but enormity also means great wickedness (the enormity of his crime).

ensure: *see* **assure**

entrée: entrée (entry) is a French word which means first course in France and in most of the rest of the world. But in the US and Americanised parts of Britain it has somehow come to mean main course.

envisage, envision: envisage, meaning foresee or plan, is common in Britain; its equivalent in the US is envision, which is also used to mean imagine or picture (she tried to envision the list she had written).

equable, equitable: equable is even-tempered; equitable is fair, just.

eschew: eschew is a literary word for avoid, shun.

evince, evoke, invoke: evince is show; evoke is draw out; invoke is call upon.

exalt, exult: to exalt is to praise; to exult is to boast.

excoriate: *see* **coruscate**

executor, executioner: an executor deals with a dead man's will and estate; an executioner kills him.

exigent, exiguous: exigent is urgent, exacting; exiguous is scanty, slender.

expatriate, ex-patriot: ex-patriot is a common mistake for expatriate (somebody who lives abroad). An 'ex-patriot' would be somebody who'd stopped loving their country whether or not they still lived there.

exponential: exponential is a literary word for increasingly rapid or steep.

exult: *see* **exalt**

farther, further: some people used to draw a distinction between farther for literal distance (five miles farther on) and further for metaphorical use (further education), but this was never generally accepted and is dying out; further and furthest are now standard in all contexts.

flammable, inflammable: both words mean easily set on fire. Flammable is now preferred by fire-prevention experts because it is unambiguous.

flaunt, flout: flaunt is show off; flout is treat with contempt.

forceful, forcible: the traditional distinction between these two is that forcible always refers to physical force (forcible entry by a burglar) whereas forceful can be metaphorical (a forceful personality).

fortuitous, fortunate: if something is fortuitous it happens by chance – and isn't necessarily a good thing. Fortunate always has the positive meaning of good luck.

fulsome: to most English speakers 'a fulsome apology' is one made without reserve; 'fulsome praise' is unstinting, emphatic. The problem with this word is that in the past it has been used to mean something different and rather subtle: excessive, insincere, cloying, disgusting by excess. So something intended as a compliment could be seen as an insult – or vice versa.

gaff, gaffe: a gaff is a hook to land a fish and to blow the gaff is to disclose a secret; a gaffe is a blunder.

gambit: a gambit is an opening move in chess which sacrifices a piece to gain an advantage, so 'opening gambit' is repetitious.

gamble, gambol: these are two kinds of play. To gamble is to risk money in a game of chance or bet on anything; to gambol is to frisk like a spring lamb.

gay: gay now means homosexual (rather than light-hearted) to almost everybody. Like the word homosexual, gay is used as both adjective and noun, but some people object to its use as a noun and insist on 'gay people' rather than 'gays'. Others (both gays and straights) seem confused about whether gay means homosexual in general or *male* homosexual (should it be 'gay men and lesbians'?). If there's any doubt, spell it out.

See also **homosexual**

genetic: *see* **congenital**

geriatric: geriatric is the adjective from geriatrics, medical care of old people. It's also a popular term of abuse for people like football referees.

gibe, gybe, jibe: to gibe is to sneer; to gybe is a nautical term meaning to change course; to jibe (with) is US usage for agree, be in accord.

gild, guild: to gild is to cover with gold; a guild is an association.

gilt, guilt: gilt is covered with gold; guilt is responsibility for wrongdoing.

gourmand, gourmet: both these French words refer to the enjoyment of food; a gourmand is inclined to be greedy, a gourmet discriminating.

graceful, gracious: graceful usually refers to physical movement though it can also mean behaving well; gracious usually refers to superior people behaving well towards their inferiors.

graffiti: graffiti, the plural of graffito, is best used with a plural verb (there were graffiti all over the walls); in the singular the word sounds strange to most people (there was a graffito on the wall).

grill, grille: to grill is to cook by radiant heat (under a grill) or to interrogate; a grille is a grating.

guild: *see* **gild**

guilt: *see* **gilt**

gybe: *see* **gibe**

hail, hale: to hail is to greet or salute (hail-fellow-well-met); to hail from is to come from; hail is frozen rain; hale is healthy (hale and hearty).

hew, hue: to hew is to chop with heavy blows; a hue is a colour or shade and also a clamour (hue-and-cry).

heyday: the heyday of something (full bloom, high point) is singular – you can't have heydays.

historic, historical: historic is important in history (a historic victory); historical is to do with history (a historical novel).

hoi polloi: hoi polloi is (ancient) Greek for the common herd. A classical scholar who's keen to be recognised as such may insist on not putting 'the' in front of this phrase on the grounds that 'hoi' is

Greek for 'the'. But they'll inevitably sound precious since not a lot of people know this. Also, since hoi polloi is sometimes misused to mean its opposite – not the plebs but the nobs – there's an argument for doing without this rather archaic expression.

holey, holy: holey is full of holes (a holey jumper); holy is saintly, religious (a holy man).

holocaust: holocaust, from the Greek *kanatos* (burnt), means huge slaughter, particularly by fire. *The* Holocaust is the mass murder of Jews by the Nazis during the second world war. Trivial use of this word is certain to cause offence.

homely: in the US homely refers to looks and means ugly; in Britain homely refers to character and means friendly, kindly. Use with care to avoid confusion and offence.

homosexual: some people are confused about the origin of this word. It comes not from *homo* (Latin, man) but from *homos* (Greek, the same), so it can refer to both men and women.

hospitalise: hospitalise is a trendy (but ugly and vague) way of saying 'send/take/admit to hospital'; it's also used to mean 'injure so the victim needs hospital treatment' (children hospitalised by school bullies).

hue: *see* hew

hummus, humus: hummus is a purée of chickpeas and sesame oil; humus is rotted organic matter used by gardeners.

immanent, imminent: immanent is inherent; imminent is about to happen.

imply, infer: *see* **mirror words** in the Grammar and style chapter

impracticable, impractical: impracticable is unable to be carried out (an impracticable scheme); impractical is a more general word which can be used about the scheme and the person proposing it (an impractical scheme/person).

inchoate, incoherent: inchoate, according to the dictionary, is 'only begun; unfinished, rudimentary; not established' (Chambers). But it is hardly ever used in this way. Most people use it as a pretentious alternative to incoherent, meaning confused (inchoate feelings).

indicate: indicate is the precise word for a car driver using indicators (he indicated left) and a rather wordy word for point out or show (he indicated the route they should follow). It's also used instead of imply, suggest, state, say etc (he indicated that he was sorry). When used in this way, it is often ambiguous: did he say he was sorry – or suggest he might be?

infer, imply: *see* **mirror words** in the Grammar and style chapter

ingenious, ingenuous: ingenious is clever; ingenuous is almost its opposite: artless, almost naïve.

insure: *see* **assure**

inter, intern: to inter is to bury; to intern is to imprison without trial.

intern, internee, internist: an intern is a trainee on work experience, particularly in the US; an internee is a person interned; an internist is a doctor specialising in internal diseases.

invoke: *see* **evince**

jibe: *see* **gibe**

judicial, judicious: judicial refers to judges and the system of justice in general; judicious is having sound judgement.

knit, knitted: knit is metaphorical (a closely knit group); knitted is literal (a knitted waistcoat).

kowtow: *see* **cow**

learn, teach: *see* **mirror words** in the Grammar and style chapter

lend, borrow: *see* **mirror words** in the Grammar and style chapter

liaison: liaison is used in cookery (eg mayonnaise) and phonetics (eg pronunciation of certain French words), of cooperation between organisations (particularly military ones) and also to refer to secret or illicit sexual relationships (he had an extramarital liaison, meaning something more than a one-night stand). Confusingly, it's also used by some people to mean a lovers' meeting. In the sexual sense it's probably clearer to use affair (he had an extramarital affair).

libel, slander: there's an important distinction here. Libel is *published* defamation (destroying a person's good name) whether in print or broadcasting or on a website; slander is spoken defamation.

lighted, lit: in Britain lit is the usual past tense (he lit the fire) and lighted the usual adjective (he used a lighted match).

liqueur, liquor: a liqueur is a sweetened, flavoured spirit (Cointreau); liquor is a general word for spirits, also used for other liquids (oysters in their own liquor).

loan: in British English loan is traditionally the noun and lend the verb but loan is increasingly used as a verb in formal agreements. Footballers and pictures are loaned by one club or gallery to another.

loath, loathe: loath is unwilling, reluctant (loath to act); to loathe is to dislike intensely.

luxuriant, luxurious, luxury: luxuriant is rich in the sense of profuse (luxuriant vegetation); luxurious is rich and lavish (a luxurious lifestyle); luxury is now increasingly common as an adjective (luxury cruise).

macerate, marinade, marinate: to macerate fruit is to soak it in alcohol and sugar; meat or fish is marinated (soaked) in a mixture of wine, vinegar, oil, herbs and spices – this mixture is a marinade.

masterful, masterly: masterful is dominating; masterly is very skilful.

meter, metre: a meter is a measuring instrument (eg a gas meter); a metre is a unit of length.

meticulous: meticulous once meant timid, then overcareful about minute details. Now it means careful, punctilious, scrupulous, precise.

militate, mitigate: to militate against something is to have a harmful effect on it (his behaviour militated against his release); to mitigate is to soften, reduce the effect of (the judge took mitigating circumstances into account).

naturalist, naturist: a naturalist studies natural history; a naturist is a nudist.

naught, nought: naught is literary for nothing (our hopes came to naught); nought is zero (a batsman is out for nought).

nauseated, nauseating, nauseous: these words come from nausea, which was originally seasickness; to be nauseated is to feel sick or be disgusted; something nauseating makes you feel sick or disgusts you. Nauseous is used to mean either nauseated or nauseating – the meal was nauseous/the meal made me (feel) nauseous.

naval, navel: naval refers to navies; navel to the belly button (hence the navel orange).

noisome: noisome has nothing to do with noise; it means disgusting.

normalcy, normality: normality is the standard word in Britain for the usual state of things; normalcy is a variation common in the US.

observance, observation: observance is observing in the sense of following, carrying out (eg a rule); observation is observing in the sense of seeing, noticing, speaking.

oculist, ophthalmologist, optometrist, optician: ophthalmologist (modern) and oculist (old-fashioned) both mean a doctor who specialises in treating eye diseases. Opticians, who supply spectacles and other optical goods, may be ophthalmic (qualified to test eyes and prescribe) or dispensing (not qualified). In the US an ophthalmic optician is called an optometrist.

official, officious: official is relating to an office (official title) or authorised (official version); officious is interfering, fussy (officious steward).

oral, verbal: the traditional distinction between these two words is that oral is spoken (oral exam) and verbal is related to words whether written or spoken (verbal reasoning). But 'verbal agreement' is the idiomatic term for something agreed but not written down.

ordinance, ordnance: an ordinance is a regulation or decree; ordnance is artillery and the supplies necessary for it.

otiose: otiose is a literary way of saying superfluous.

pace: pace (from the Latin, pronounced parché) is a literary way of disagreeing with somebody politely and formally.

paean, paeon, peon, peony: a paean, originally a song, is now literary for any form of praise; a paeon is a metrical foot in classical poetry; a peon is a peasant or similar in Latin America or India; a peony is a flower.

palate, palette, pallet: the palate is the roof of the mouth and so the sense of taste (she has an excellent palate); a palette is the board on which a painter mixes colour and so the range of colours; a pallet is a platform for moving and storing goods and also a mattress.

pants: pants is both short for underpants (in Britain) and a common word for trousers (particularly in the US); it's also slang for nonsense, rubbish.

paparazzo: paparazzo is the singular of paparazzi. As with graffito/i the plural form is more familiar.

parameter, perimeter: parameter is a technical term in maths, referring to a variable factor constant in a particular case. It is often used as a trendy alternative to limit or boundary (keep expenditure inside agreed parameters), possibly through confusion with perimeter (boundary).

partially, partly: partially is not fully (he is partially blind); partly is in part (the house was partly painted).

pathos: *see* **bathos**

pedagogy, pedantry: pedagogy is the art or science of teaching; pedantry is excessive concern for trifling details, eg of language.

pedal, peddle: to pedal is to ride (a bicycle); to peddle is to sell goods from place to place. A travelling vendor is a pedlar in Britain but somebody selling drugs is a peddler.

perimeter: *see* **parameter**

perspicacious, perspicuous: perspicacious is literary for astute, perspicuous for clear.

pertain: pertain is literary for belong, apply.

peruse: peruse is literary for read carefully – and read without qualification. But the problems don't end there: peruse is also used to mean examine, check, revise.

petrel, petrol: a petrel is a seabird; petrol (from petroleum) is fuel for cars.

poof, pouf, pouff, pouffe: poof is a derogatory word for a male homosexual (other similar ones are poove and poofter); pouf is recommended (rather than pouff or pouffe) for a large firm cushion with a solid base, a type of hairstyle or the padded part of a dress.

populace, populous: the populace is literary for ordinary people; populous (of a place) means heavily populated.

pore, pour: to pore (over) is to examine closely; to pour is to stream or allow to stream (eg tea).

portentous, pretentious: portentous can be either ominous (a portentous event) or pompous (his portentous attitude); pretentious means pretending to be important.

poser, poseur: a poser is somebody who poses in the literal sense (eg an artist's model) and also a puzzle; a poseur is somebody who strikes false attitudes.

possibly: *see* arguably

pour: *see* pore

practicable, practical: practicable is able to be carried out (a practicable scheme); practical is a more general word which can be used about the scheme and the person proposing it (a practical scheme/person).

precipitate, precipitous: precipitate is literary for sudden, hasty, rash; precipitous is steep (like a precipice).

premier, premiere: premier as a noun is prime minister and as an adjective is foremost; a premiere is the first public showing of a film.

prescribe, proscribe: to prescribe is to lay down or specify (a doctor prescribes medicine); to proscribe is to forbid or condemn (a doctor proscribes smoking).

presumptive, presumptuous: presumptive is giving grounds for presuming (a presumptive heir); presumptuous is presuming too much, so insolent.

prevaricate, procrastinate: to prevaricate is to speak or act evasively or misleadingly; to procrastinate is to delay.

pristine: pristine, traditionally original, ancient, primitive, is a vogue word used to mean clean, unspoilt, unused (when it's cleared up the place will look pristine).

probably: *see* **arguably**

protagonist: traditionally, the protagonist (from Greek drama) is the chief actor; there is only one (so 'chief protagonist' is nonsense). But the word is now used to mean participant in general, one of two people fighting each other, supporter of a particular cause etc.

psych, psyche: psych is the informal abbreviation for psychologist (eg ed psych); psyche is soul, spirit, mind.

qua: qua is literary for 'as' meaning in the capacity, character or role of (money qua money can't buy me love).

quaff: quaff is literary for both drink – and drink in large draughts.

quite: quite has several contrasting meanings: quite good is less than good; quite excellent is as excellent as it could be; and as a response to something said 'Quite' means exactly.

ravage, ravish: to ravage is to devastate, lay waste, destroy; to ravish can be to rape and also to enchant, enrapture, entrance – hence the adjective ravishing (delightful).

raze: to raze (or rase) a building is to demolish it, so there is no need to add 'to the ground'.

rebut, refute: refute is more common than rebut but these words present essentially the same problem. They have a traditional meaning, still insisted on by usage guides and stylebooks, and a popular use, which is very different. Both rebut and refute are used by most people to mean deny – but this irritates purists and causes confusion. To be clear use either disprove or deny instead.

register not **registry** office for weddings.

regretful, regrettable: regretful is feeling or showing regret; regrettable is causing it (his conduct was regrettable and he is now regretful).

regularly: regularly is often used to mean often (it rains regularly in April) but it can also have its traditional meaning of at regular intervals (the house is cleaned regularly).

rehearse: rehearse, practise beforehand (what actors do), is also used as a trendy alternative to discuss (questions of sexuality are endlessly rehearsed).

repertoire, repertory: a repertoire is the list of items that a person or company can perform; a repertory company is a theatre company with a repertoire of plays.

replete: replete is literary for full, stuffed; it is also used by mistake instead of complete (with), meaning 'having as an important accompaniment' (they built a discovery centre replete with coffee shop and crèche).

reticent, reluctant: reticent is reserved, reluctant to speak; reluctant is unwilling to act in general. Some people now use reticent as though it meant reluctant – which leads to nonsense like 'Men are reticent to talk about their diseases.'

reverend, reverent: reverend is deserving reverence and is used as a title for clergy, eg the Rev(erend) Jane Smith; reverent is showing reverence.

riffle, rifle: to riffle through, eg the pages of a book, is to make a casual search; to rifle something is to ransack it.

saccharin, saccharine: saccharin is a substitute for sugar; saccharine means sugary, both literally and metaphorically.

salon, saloon: a salon is a French living or reception room, particularly a grand one, a social gathering (eg of writers) in such a room and the place where hairdressers and beauticians operate. A saloon is a public room on a ship and a bar in the US, particularly in westerns.

salubrious, salutary, sanitary: these words all refer to health but are used differently. Salubrious is literary for healthy and pleasant to live in (a salubrious district); salutary is mainly metaphorical and means beneficial (he learnt a salutary lesson); sanitary is used of cleanliness, freedom from infection and public health.

sari, sarong: a sari is the Hindu woman's traditional garment; a sarong is a length of cloth worn as a skirt by men and women in Malaysia and Polynesia.

scallop, escalope: a scallop (not scollop or escallop) is a shellfish, a shallow pan and decorative edging; an escalope is a thin boneless slice of meat.

scan: scan can be glance at or examine carefully or (of verse) conform to the rules of metre.

seasonable, seasonal: seasonable is appropriate to the season; seasonal is a more general adjective meaning in season, characteristic of the seasons or a particular one.

sensual, sensuous: the traditional distinction between these two words is that sensual implies physical, usually sexual, gratification whereas sensuous relates to the senses in general. But the distinction is widely ignored.

sewage, sewerage: sewage is waste; sewerage is the system of sewers which disposes of it.

silicon, silicone: silicon is a chemical element used in electrical components (silicon chip); silicone is a derivative of silicon used as a lubricant, an adhesive and a breast implant.

slander: *see* libel

stanch, staunch: to stanch is to stop the flow of something, eg blood; staunch is loyal.

stile, style: a stile is steps over a fence; style is the way things are done.

stimulant, stimulus: a stimulant is a drug; a stimulus is everything else that stimulates, ie produces a response in a living organism or encourages increased activity.

straight, strait: these words are not related though they are often confused. As an adjective straight is uncurved, direct, normal; as a noun it's the last part of a racecourse, a heterosexual etc; as an adverb it's directly (go straight home). Strait as an adjective is narrow; as a noun it's a narrow place or passage, particularly at sea, and a difficulty.

syndrome: a syndrome is a cluster of medical symptoms not a single problem or defect.

systematic, systemic: systematic is methodical and thorough (a systematic search); systemic is affecting the system or body as a whole (a systemic pesticide).

tactile: the traditional meaning of tactile is relating to touch, and then pleasing to the touch (a tactile piece of furniture). It is also a vogue word meaning something like 'having wandering hands' in the sexual sense (as the drinks flowed, he became increasingly tactile).

titillate, titivate: to titillate is to excite, almost always sexually (titillating nude drawings); to titivate is to smarten up.

ton, tonne, tun: a tonne is a metric ton and slightly heavier than an imperial ton; a tun is a large cask for beer, wine or cider.

torpid, torrid: torpid is sluggish; torrid is violently hot.

tortuous, torturous: tortuous is winding, circuitous; torturous is causing torture, painful.

troop: a troop is a body of soldiers not an individual; the plural 'troops' is used in a general sense (bring the troops home).

urban, urbane: urban is of or belonging to a city; urbane is refined and courteous.

use, utilise: use is the ordinary word for make use of (he used a saucepan, use your head etc); utilise is a pompous way of saying the same thing (he utilised a saucepan – that's bad enough but utilise your head?).

venal, venial: venal is able to be bought, corrupt (a venal official); venial is minor, excusable (a venial sin).

verbal: *see* **oral**

vest: as with **pants** there is the risk of confusion between British and American usage. In Britain a vest is underwear; in the US it's what Brits call a waistcoat.

waive, wave: to waive is to give up or refrain from taking (he waived his claim to the land); to wave is to move the hand in greeting.

waiver, waver: a waiver is the giving-up of a claim; to waver is to hesitate or falter.

wastage, waste: wastage is loss resulting from use or natural causes; waste can imply criticism (wasting water is squandering it).

4
Punctuation

As more and more words are typed every day on computer keyboards, laptops, mobile phones and so on, the point of punctuation is increasingly obvious: it helps writers get their message across clearly and emphatically. The faster and more frenetic the pace of communication, the more critical it is to organise what you write and make it clear. If you don't bother with punctuation you risk being misunderstood – maybe even ignored. Post a great wodge of unpunctuated text on a website in the middle of a series of pithy comments and people are likely to scroll down past your message to the next one that's easily understood.

Print – books, newspapers, magazines, brochures, leaflets, greetings cards and so on – is emphatically not a dying medium. In fact everybody with access to a computer keyboard and a printer can now be their own desktop publisher and produce reports, essays, leaflets, posters, newsletters . . .

But what makes print work so well in principle – clarity, regularity, uniformity – also draws attention to minor mistakes and inconsistencies that are hardly noticeable in something written by hand. What's printed has to aim to look professional or it will certainly look amateur – careless and slapdash. It has to be punctuated properly in the broadest sense, which implies using appropriate headings and typefaces. And it has to follow a coherent house style – a consistent way of spelling, punctuating, emphasising and so on.

Punctuation practice is constantly changing. For example, sentences are much shorter than they used to be, so now there are more full stops. At its worst this trend breaks a sentence into two – leaving a subordinate clause as a new stand-alone sentence (the one beginning 'Because'):

> But the film also reminds us that his times are not our times. Because Kinsey lived in an age that could be straightforwardly optimistic about the rewards offered by sexual frankness.

There's no problem with putting a conjunction like 'but' or 'and' at the beginning of a sentence. But there is certainly a problem with 'because' here: it introduces a subordinate clause not followed by a main clause – there's no proper sentence. So the reader is likely to stumble and have to reread the passage, mentally overriding the full stop.

Incomplete sentences like the one quoted are called fragments (see p. 64). As in this example, they can be longer than a complete sentence – which only makes the problem worse.

The reverse mistake – running two sentences together joined by a comma – is called the comma splice (see the Comma below).

There's a clear trend in fiction and journalism to punctuate quoted speech with commas – suggesting informality, spontaneity – where logic and clarity would demand stronger stops. And in turn the commas are disappearing from all sorts of places like dates, addresses, the beginnings and ends of letters.

In general, there is less punctuation now. Most people no longer use full stops after abbreviations. Capital letters, once used for expressions like the Continent (of Europe as seen from Britain), the Church and the Chancellor of the Exchequer, are now much less common. Apostrophes hardly ever mark plurals; dos and don'ts, which started out with three apostrophes (do's and don't's), lost the third one, then the first – and now has only one.

Indeed some people, following George Bernard Shaw, would prefer not to bother with apostrophes at all: they'd prefer dont to don't and theyd to they'd. In private emails anything goes. But the apostrophe is still necessary in public writing.

The hyphen is on the retreat. Some previously hyphenated words like wicket-keeper and e-mail have become single words. In other cases people drop the hyphen but keep the two words separate. So nowadays you often see a phrase like single issue campaign where single-issue campaign would be more easily understood. This is irritating in text – and can seriously mislead in newspaper headlines.

Again following Shaw, some newspapers and magazines no longer put the titles of books, plays, films etc into italics. But then again others do. At the *Guardian* the main newspaper doesn't use italics for titles while the Saturday book-review section does.

In general, the policy in this chapter is to try to give sensible advice on punctuation without either trying to turn the clock back to 1900 or endorsing the latest fad. There is no attempt to be exhaustive – but the main points are covered. (For specialist books on punctuation, see Further reading.) In what follows the four main stops are the **comma**, the **semicolon**, the **colon** and the **full stop**. Of these the comma is the weakest and the full stop the strongest: it ends a sentence whereas the other three mark pauses in it.

The colon used to be seen as a stronger stop than the semicolon. Now the semicolon lies midway between a comma and a full stop while the colon has a series of specialist uses.

The **paragraph break** could be called the fifth main stop since it's one stage stronger than the full stop. As with other forms of punctuation its main purpose is to make reading easier. A new paragraph can signal a change of subject or give the reader a breather.

Paragraphs are shorter now than they used to be. It follows that most readers expect to read short ones and are likely to be put off by long ones.

The **question mark** and the **exclamation mark** are alternative ways of ending a sentence. They show that it asks a question or expresses strong emotion – amazement, shock, horror etc. The exclamation mark can also be used for emphasis in general – as can a whole range of things discussed below: **bold** and *italic* type, **underlining**, **capitals** and different typefaces.

For direct quotation, writers use either single or double **quotes**, while quoted text can also be indented (to a narrower width) or set in different type. Omission of words in quotations is shown by three dots, and omission of parts of words is shown by the **apostrophe**, which also marks possession. Insertion of words into quotations, on the other hand, is shown by **square brackets**.

For text which is not quoted there are various ways of marking a parenthesis – from a simple pair of commas to show somebody's age or title, by way of **dashes** for emphasis, to **round brackets** (also confusingly called parentheses).

Dashes, which punctuate sentences, must be distinguished from **hyphens**, which join one word to another. Then there are punctuation marks and signs with various specialist uses: **slashes** (which go by at least half-a-dozen other names), **asterisks, accents, bullet points** . . . not to mention **numbers, fractions and dates**.

Accents, accent marks, diacritics

Accents, or accent marks (or to be pedantic, diacritics), should generally be kept in a word taken from another language if they show how it is pronounced. Common accent marks are: the acute (é), the grave (à), the cedilla (ç) and the circumflex (ô) from French; the tilde (ñ) from Spanish; and the umlaut (ü) from German – which is identical to the diaeresis/dieresis (see below).

So keep the acute accent on common words of French origin like café, cliché, entrée and soirée where the accent shows the sound of the word: cliché ('clich-ay') as opposed to clique ('cleek'); entrée ('on-tray') as opposed to trainee ('train-ee'). Other familiar words taken from French – elite, regime, role and premiere – have tended to lose their accents as they are increasingly seen as serving no purpose in English.

If you put one accent on a foreign word to show its pronunciation, you must logically include any other accents it has. So pâté needs its circumflex and résumé (summary as opposed to start again) needs its first acute accent as well as its second.

Diaeresis/dieresis (¨) – double dots on top of a letter to show that two successive vowels are sounded separately – is on its way out in ordinary English writing (naive, naively, naivety not naïve etc). But people whose parents called them Chloë or Noël usually prefer to keep the double dots (and having an exotic accent on top of their surname didn't seem to do the Brontë sisters any harm).

The grave accent once put on words like learnèd and agèd, to show how to pronounce them, has disappeared from modern publishing.

Acute accent – *see* **Accents**
Angle brackets – *see* **Brackets**

Apostrophe

The apostrophe (') has three uses:

1   to show that something is left out of a word:

    don't (do not)
    rock 'n' roll (and)

2   to mark the possessive:

    the woman's job (the job done by the woman)
    the children's books (the books read by the children)

3   where absolutely necessary, to mark a plural:

mind your p's and q's
the word receive has three e's

But it's better to use variations in type such as caps or italic:

mind your Ps and Qs/mind your *ps* and *qs*

Apostrophes are now rarely used to show that a word has been shortened, so avoid putting them in front of phone or after deli. Try to avoid things like 'the '60s' (prefer the 1960s in full or, if necessary, the sixties). And always avoid the so-called greengrocer's apostrophe (ridiculed by, among others, Keith Waterhouse and Lynne Truss):

tom's 40p

Common apostrophe problems include:

1   Singular or plural? Is it the bee's or the bees' knees, the cat's or the cats' whiskers, a doll's or a dolls' house?

    Solution: in almost every case common expressions like these take the singular. When in doubt check the dictionary.

2   Place names – some have apostrophes; some don't (King's Langley but Kings Norton).

    Solution: follow usage; when in doubt use a reference book.

3   Names of organisations – some have apostrophes; some don't (Harrods but Christie's).

    Solution: follow the organisation's own style (check their website or the phone directory) unless it is unarguably illiterate: for example, don't write 'Mens' ', 'Womens' or 'Childrens' ' incorrectly even if they do.

4   The extra 's': Thomas' or Thomas's?

Solution: follow sound – if the extra 's' is sounded, include it:

St Thomas's hospital, Marx's theories

But if there's no extra 's' in speech, don't add one in writing:

Degas' art, Socrates' philosophy

5   How many apostrophes in a double possessive?

Fred and Mary's house is mortgaged up to the hilt.

Solution: where Fred and Mary own a house together, they need only one apostrophe. But if each of them owns a house, a second apostrophe is needed:

Fred's and Mary's houses are both heavily mortgaged.

6   The double apostrophe, as in:

Fred's book's title

Solution: avoid it where possible, so prefer:

the title of Fred's book

7   The apostrophe with a title in single quotes:

the point of 'Ode to Autumn's' imagery

Solution: either don't use quotes for titles or prefer:

the point of the imagery of 'Ode to Autumn'

Asterisk, star

The star-shaped asterisk (*), which is sometimes called a star, has numerous uses including:

1   as a guide to a footnote (both in the text and before the footnote):

This is crazy.*

* But not everybody agrees.

2   as a device to show that certain letters have been omitted:

you stupid b*****

3   in dictionaries and reference books to mark a non-standard usage (eg a US spelling in a British dictionary):

favour n. Also *favor

4   in modern linguistic writing to mark an example of 'wrong' language:

*Leave the room, kindly. (for Kindly leave the room.)

The asterisk is also used in various specialist fields such as computing, mathematics and philology.

Bar – *see* Slash
Blob – *see* Bullet point

Bold

Boldface type (now just bold) is a thicker form of a particular type-face. **This is bold.** It is used for headings and for strong emphasis.

Brace brackets – *see* Brackets

Brackets, round, square, angle, brace

There are four main types of bracket: round brackets ( ), also called parentheses, particularly in the US, square brackets [ ] – just brackets in the US – angle brackets < > and brace or curly brackets { }.

Use **round brackets** for routine parenthesis, where something stronger than a comma is needed; that is for any digressions, explanations, translations, abbreviations (or full forms of abbreviations), references etc that you, the writer, add to your original text:

1 Last Monday (it was his birthday as it happens) Fred was knocked over by a car.
2 He was walking quickly and a bit carelessly (he was already late for work).

3   While he was lying in the road somebody said 'Il est blessé.' (That's French for he's injured.)
4   He was taken to the hospital's accident and emergency (A & E) department.
5   He went to A & E (accident and emergency).
6   The story was in the local paper (page 9).

Note the punctuation. In examples 1 and 2 a complete sentence is included in the brackets with no extra punctuation. But in 3 the bracketed sentence has its own capital letter and full stop. Example 2 could also be punctuated as follows:

He was walking quickly and a bit carelessly. (He was already late for work.)

Use **square brackets** for any digressions etc which you, the writer, add to somebody else's written or spoken text when you quote it:

1   'Last Monday [it was his birthday as it happens] Fred was knocked over by a car.'
2   'He was walking quickly and a bit carelessly [he was already late for work].'

In the US (but not in Britain) square brackets are also used for parentheses within parentheses.

Angle brackets are used in works on the English language to supply text that is missing, defective or illegible and also in linguistics. **Brace or curly brackets** are used to enclose alternatives.

Bullet point, blob

Bullet points, also called blobs, particularly in journalism, are used to emphasise the various items (particularly short ones) in a list:

- like this
- and this

They can also be used at the beginning of a new paragraph to show that it has been added on to the main text.

Solid squares and arrows can be used in the same way.

Capitals, caps, upper case

There is constant change in the use of capital letters – and it tends to be away from caps towards lower case. Trendy businesses give themselves titles without caps; internet companies do without them in their website addresses; email users and bloggers follow suit; in their house style newspapers and magazines reflect the trend and reinforce it . . . so it's increasingly difficult to be prescriptive about where caps must be used.

In ordinary writing caps are used as follows:

1   To start sentences:

He made a speech.

2   To start sentences that are quoted in full inside quote marks:

He said: 'She's waiting for you outside.'

Note that incomplete quotes don't start with caps:

He said she was waiting 'outside'.

3   To start exclamations:

I went outside. Wow! She was there.

4   To start almost anything that is written – letters, addresses, individual lines of poetry, points in a list etc:

Dear Fred

5   For names, eg of individual people (George Smith), nations (the French), religions (Quakers), languages (Spanish), places (Rome), months (February) and days of the week (Tuesday).

6   For titles, eg of individual people (the Duke of Edinburgh) and works of art (the Mona Lisa).

Caret

The caret mark ^ is used to show omission. It may be used intentionally by the writer or by somebody else (an editor or proofreader, for example, as a note to writer or printer):

He was picked for the ^ team.

The missing word(s) can then be added either in the margin (which is recommended) or above the caret mark if there's space:

football
He was picked for the ^ team.

Cedilla – *see* Accents
Circumflex – *see* Accents

Colon

1   Colons are more emphatic than commas so use them to introduce full-sentence quotes:

He said: 'Punctuation is difficult.'

But don't use them – or commas – when you quote only a word or phrase:

She said she found punctuation 'very easy'.

In continuous dialogue (eg plays) the quote marks are left out:

FRED: What did you say?
SALLY: Not a lot.

2   Use colons to introduce examples and lists:

They were all invited: Bill, Jack, Ted and Willie.

The style of this book is to use colons in this way.

3   Use colons between sentences where the second explains or justifies the first:

Keep your language uncluttered: it will read more easily.

4   Colons can be used between two sentences to emphasise a strong contrast:

Man proposes: God disposes.

5   Colons are used between a title and a subtitle:

The Book of Psalms: A Translation with Commentary

6   Colons are used for emphasis and economy in headlines and picture captions:

Needed: an England backbone
Sharapova: victorious

7   Colons are used in writing the time, particularly in the US, and in digital clocks:

5:30pm
17:30

8   In the US colons are sometimes used at the beginning of letters:

Dear Sir:

9   Colons are also used in indexes and biblical and bibliographical references, and have special uses in mathematics and the sciences.

Comma

Most uses of the comma can be described as linking (joining elements of a list, connecting a main clause with a subordinate one), separating (marking a weak parenthesis) or marking omission.

The comma is used extensively in the punctuation of quotes – see **Quote marks**. Many people also use commas (rather than colons) to introduce quotes – but colons are more emphatic and increasingly preferred in publishing.

Commas are no longer used by most people in dates and addresses.

1 Use commas between words of the same kind where you would otherwise use 'and' or 'or':

You should write clear, concise, accurate English./You should write clear, concise and accurate English.

(In each case the meaning is the same: your English should be clear and concise and accurate.)

You should write in English, French, Spanish or German.
(. . . English or French or Spanish or German)

We asked the butcher, the baker and the candlestick-maker.
(. . . the butcher and the baker and the candlestick-maker)

2 But don't use commas when a series of adjectives is cumulative, where you would not otherwise use 'and':

He ordered a rich chocolate sponge cake.

Punctuation

(You couldn't say the cake was rich and chocolate and sponge: it was a sponge cake, which was chocolate-flavoured; the chocolate, or possibly the cake, was rich.)

She was wearing a bright blue swimming costume.

(Her swimming costume was bright blue.)

3   Use commas between phrases of the same kind:

His writing was more refined, more intellectual and more complex than Smith's.

They looked in the filing cabinet, on the mantelpiece and under the bookcase.

4   Use a comma before the 'and' at the end of a list where it is necessary to make the sentence clear and easily readable:

The menu is soup, fish and chips, and trifle.

(It's a three-course meal; the chips come with the fish not the trifle.)

The guests were Kit and Jemima, Wendy and Rick, and Humphrey.

(Rick came with Wendy not Humphrey, who came by himself.) But don't use a comma where it isn't necessary:

The menu is soup, fish, and trifle.
The guests were Kit, Rick, and Humphrey.

This 'serial comma' after 'fish' and 'Rick', also called the 'Oxford comma' because the Oxford University Press traditionally

158

favours it, is not normal practice in British English unless it is necessary for readability. But in the US it is considered essential.

5   Use a comma between three or more clauses or sentences when they form a sequence or list:

I came, I saw, I conquered.
Fred speaks French, Eric speaks German, I speak Dutch.

Note that you could also use semicolons instead:

Fred speaks French; Eric speaks German; I speak Dutch.

In fact the longer the items, the stronger the case for semicolons.

6   Use a comma to mark off words that address somebody or something:

Come on, City!
Sir, are you serious?

7   Use a comma, where appropriate, to mark off words or phrases like 'however', 'for example', 'in fact', 'of course':

However, with punctuation it pays to be careful.
I am, of course, open to argument.

8   Use commas to mark off a word or phrase in a weak parenthesis. In the example below the word 'Arkansas' is in parenthesis – you can read across it, and the sentence would make sense without it.

Born in Little Rock, Arkansas, Bill Clinton became president of the US.

Norman Mailer's first novel, *The Naked and the Dead*, was a bestseller.

The sentence 'Norman Mailer's first novel was a bestseller' would make sense without the title being given. Commas round it show that you can read across it.

But don't use commas where the phrase is essential to the meaning of the sentence:

Norman Mailer's novel *The Naked and the Dead* was a bestseller.

In this example giving the title – without commas – tells the reader which of Mailer's novels was a bestseller. Putting commas round the title would suggest that Mailer had written only one novel ('Norman Mailer's novel . . . was a bestseller').

9 Use commas to mark off a clause in parenthesis:

The students, who were in their shirtsleeves, worked fast.

Again the sentence 'The students worked fast' would make sense without the incidental information about their clothes – we're talking about all the students here.

But don't use commas when the clause is essential to the meaning of the sentence:

The students who were in their shirtsleeves worked fast; those who kept their jackets on worked more slowly.

10 Use a comma, where necessary, to mark off an introductory phrase or clause:

Because of the appalling weather, conditions for holidaymakers were intolerable.

Here the comma makes the sentence easier to read by separating 'weather' from 'conditions'.

Where a phrase or clause that used to need a pair of commas follows a conjunction like 'but' or 'and', the first one is now rare:

Fred tried to get up but [,] because he was tired and emotional, he failed.

11 Use a comma where two sentences are joined by a conjunction if you want to lengthen the pause:

He wanted to leave the meeting, but his friend stopped him.

Don't use a comma where you want a short pause or where the subject of the two sentences is the same:

He wanted to leave but didn't.

12 In general, don't use commas between sentences where there is no conjunction. Avoid this kind of thing:

He wanted to leave the meeting, his friend stopped him.

This way of joining two sentences is called the 'comma splice'. It's used by various reputable writers, above all in recording speech, but if you do try to follow their example, you risk confusing your reader. The semicolon would be better here because it would make clear that these are two separate sentences.

13 In the same way words like however and nevertheless combined with commas should not be used to splice sentences:

He wanted to leave the meeting, however, his friend stopped him.

As well as running the two sentences together this example gives the reader an extra headache: which way to read 'however'? Does it refer to the first part of the sentence or the second?

14 Use a comma, where necessary, to show that words have been left out of a sentence (to avoid unnecessary repetition). A comma is used in the following quotation from Alexander Pope:

> To err is human; to forgive, divine.

But many people would not bother to put a comma in this sentence:

> Some people drink too much; others too little.

Dagger, obelisk

The dagger (†), also called the obelisk, is used as a guide to a footnote (both in the text and before the footnote):

> I told you this was crazy.†

Dash

Printers and publishers traditionally distinguish between the en dash (–), so-called because it's the width of the letter 'n', and the em dash

† But nobody listened.

(−), the width of the letter 'm'. This book – like most of those published in Britain – uses the en dash with a space either side, whereas most US publishers prefer the unspaced em dash.

An extra-long dash was often used in Victorian novels to avoid being explicit (d——d for damned, S—— for Sussex). It can still be found in newspapers to preserve anonymity (Darren ——) and in book lists for repetitions of an author's name (often 2 ems: see Further reading).

1   Use dashes to mark a strong, emphatic parenthesis:

The burglar lived nearby – just across the road – all the time he was planning the break-in.

2   In general use the dash to add emphasis or mark a surprise:

This is the point – there's no getting away from it.
Guess who came to dinner – Jane Grigson.

3   Use the dash to mark a change of direction or interruption, particularly in speech:

'I suppose – but what's the use of supposing?'
'I suppose – ' 'Why are you always supposing?'

4   Use the dash, where appropriate, to introduce an explanation or a list or to sum up:

Oranges, bananas, strawberries – I like all kinds of fruit.
I like all sorts of fruit – oranges, bananas, strawberries.

Note that here the colon would do as well – but the dash is looser, less formal.

5 Use the dash in a range of numbers, particularly dates, and to show other close links between things, particularly places. 'A–B' means 'from A to B'/'between A and B':

The flight takes 10–12 hours.
(between 10 and 12 hours)

He was born during the 1914–18 war.
(the war fought from 1914 to 1918 or between 1914 and 1918)

He's taking the London–Paris train.
(the train from London to Paris)

Don't mix up the two styles. So don't write:

The flight takes between 10–12 hours./He's going from London–Paris.

Since '10–12 hours' means 'between 10 and 12 hours', you have effectively written:

The flight takes between between 10 and 12 hours.

Since 'London–Paris' means 'from London to Paris', you've written:

He's going from from London to Paris.

Diaeresis/Dieresis – *see* **Accents**
Diagonal – *see* **Slash**

Ditto marks

Ditto marks (″) are used to avoid having to write the same thing several times:

The winner of the first semifinal will play
     ″   second semifinal in the final.

Keep ditto marks for informal writing.

Dots, ellipsis, leader dots

1   Use three dots to show that something has been omitted from a quotation:

'Oats. A grain, which . . . is generally given to horses, but in Scotland supports the people.'

2   Use three dots to mark a trailing off, interruption or pause in speech or thought:

I suppose . . . but what's the use of supposing?

Note that the dash is used for more abrupt interruptions.

3   Use three dots to suggest that a sequence is unfinished:

They had course after course – soup, hors d'oeuvre, fish, meat . . .

4   Most writers and publishers no longer add a full stop after three dots to mark the end of a sentence – but if a question mark or exclamation mark is needed it follows the three dots:

    Could they finish the endless meal – soup, hors d'oeuvre, fish, meat . . .?

5   Use lines of dots in charts and tables to make them more read-able.

Double dots – *see* **Accents**
Ellipsis – *see* **Dots**

Exclamation mark, screamer, shriek

Use the exclamation mark (known to journalists as a screamer) only when necessary to mark an exclamation:

    'Ooh, I say!'
    'Come on, City!'

'What' and 'how' often introduce exclamations:

    What a fool I was!/How foolish I was!

Unless you want to sound hysterical (or at least breathless) don't use the exclamation mark to make comments, signal jokes or mark rhetorical questions (which need question marks). And – except to parody the American writer Tom Wolfe (famous for his playful punc-tuation) – never, please, follow one exclamation mark by another.

Full stop, full point, period

Use the full stop to mark the end of a sentence that isn't a question or exclamation. Full stops are no longer necessary to mark abbreviations, although some people continue to use them. They are still used in the following cases:

1   In figures including decimals: 7.5 per cent
2   Between units of money: £5.50, €10.25
3   In British English between hours and minutes: 5.30pm; 17.30 (US English uses colons: 5:30pm; 17:30)
4   In website and email addresses: www.routledge.com, wynford@hicksinfrance.net

See also **Dots**

Grave – *see* **Accents**

Hash

The hash or hash mark (#) is used to mean 'number' in street addresses, particularly in the US:

1627 Fairmount Avenue

Hyphen

Use the hyphen in compound words where it clarifies the meaning:

1   For a title:

    vice-president

2   For prefix plus adjective:

    extra-curricular activities

3   For adjective plus adjective:

    red-hot coals

    The first adjective modifies the second.

4   For adverb plus adjective used before the noun:

    a well-known fact

    but

    The fact is well known.

    There is no need for a hyphen after adverbs ending in -ly because their meaning is clear. So whereas:

    a close-knit band of men

    needs a hyphen,

a closely knit band of men

does not.

5   For adjective plus noun:

a black-cab driver

This refers to the driver of a black cab (which in London means an officially licensed cab). By contrast 'black cab driver' may suggest that the driver is black.

6   For noun plus noun:

a black cab-driver

This does make it clear that the driver, rather than the cab, is black.

7   For noun plus preposition plus noun:

mother-in-law

8   For verb plus adverb used as a noun:

get-together

When used as a verb the word does not take the hyphen:

We get together (at a get-together).

9   For prefix plus proper noun or adjective:

pre-Christian

10 For prefix plus word to distinguish between meanings:

re-creation (making something again)
recreation (leisure)

11 For two words that together make a clumsy or ugly juxtaposition:

supra-intestinal
Caithness-shire

12 For figures written out:

seventy-six

13 For word breaks at the end of lines.

Note that with unjustified setting (uneven right-hand margins) hyphens are less common. Avoid a succession of word breaks. When you hyphenate, try to break words into their constituent parts.

Italics

Italic type (italics, itals) slopes to the right *like this*. Italics are used:

1 For emphasis:

What did you say?

2 To refer to phrases, words or parts of words:

Expressions like *the reason is because* are illiterate and should be avoided.
Some feminists object to the word *actress*.
Combated is spelt with only one *t*.

3   For the titles of books, films, newspapers, TV programmes etc:

The magazine *Time Out* publishes reviews of plays (*Hamlet*), films (*Pulp Fiction*) and TV programmes (*Life on Mars*).

4   For the names of ships, aircraft, spacecraft etc:

Nelson's flagship *Victory* is in Portsmorth.

5   For foreign words and phrases that remain unfamiliar in English:

There is a *prima facie* case for italicising a word like *schaden-freude* – and anyway it looks foreign.

6   For scientific names:

Quercus robur (the oak tree) can be abbreviated to *Q robur*.

Numbers, fractions, dates

1   Conventions vary but a good modern style (the *Guardian*'s) is to spell out numbers from one to nine with figures starting at 10. But don't mix letters and figures: instead of 'nine-10' go for '9–10'.

And it's a well-established convention that you don't start a sentence with a figure; so not:

'15 people were at the meeting.'

but

'Fifteen people were at the meeting.'

or

'There were 15 people at the meeting.'

2   Some people (in Britain but not often in the US) put a comma in four-digit figures:

1,000; 3,679; 5,789

But dates never have commas:

1942; 1984; 2000

3   In both countries commas are necessary where figures have five or more digits:

43,078; 546,980; 2,094,459

But in technical writing spaces replace commas:

43 078; 546 980; 2 094 459 etc

4   The best style for abbreviations of such things as heights, weights, measures and large sums of money is figure plus short form with no space:

£10m; 5ft tall; 5lb/2kg

5 Where possible, spell out fractions in text:

two-thirds, three-quarters, four-fifths

But in tables etc prefer $^2/_3$, $^3/_4$, $^4/_5$

6 Commas and 'st/th' are no longer needed in dates:

20 March 1942

(not 20th March, 1942)

Since American publishers (and some British ones) reverse the day-month order, always write the date in full if there is any risk of confusion. In general avoid:

20/3/1942 and 3/20/1942

For punctuation of ranges of numbers see **Dash**.

Obelisk – *see* **Dagger**
Oblique – *see* **Slash**

Paragraph break

The most common way of marking a paragraph break in printed text is by indenting (starting the new paragraph on a new line a few spaces in from the edge of the page).

Like this.

The alternative is to leave a line space between one paragraph and the next.

Note that where new paragraphs are indented the first paragraph of a new chapter or section is not indented but set full out:

Like this.

Parentheses – *see* **Brackets**

Question mark, query

1   Use the question mark after a direct question in or out of quotes:

What time is it?
He asked: 'What time is it?'

The question can be abbreviated to a single word:

Name? (for What is your name?)

2   Don't use a question mark after an indirect question:

He asked me what time it was.

3   A rhetorical question – one that doesn't expect an answer – should still have a question mark:

Why is everybody always picking on me?

4   A tag question (a question tagged onto a statement) should have a question mark:

He would say that, wouldn't he?

5   A question that is put in the form of a statement should have a question mark:

You won't stay? I can't get you to change your mind?

6   But a request in the form of a question does not need one:

Would all those who have difficulty with punctuation please buy this book.

7   A question mark is also used to show uncertainty about names, dates, spellings etc:

Joan of Arc (?1412–31)

Quote marks, quotes, inverted commas

Quotation marks, whether single (' ') or double (" "), are nowadays better known as quote marks or quotes, though some people still refer to inverted commas (but please not 'speech marks', which is nursery-school speak). This book uses single quotes as standard, as do many British publishers, while in the US (and sometimes in Britain) double quotes are standard. Invariably, quotes within quotes take the alternative form: single inside double; double inside single; and so on.

Some British publishers used to make a distinction between double quote marks for speech and single quote marks for other purposes (as in 6, 7 and 8 below). And Lynne Truss in her famous punctuation book *Eats, Shoots & Leaves* seems to want to revive the distinction. She writes:

> There is a difference between saying someone is "out of sorts" (a direct quote) and 'out of sorts' (i.e., not feeling very well): when single quotes serve both functions, you lose this distinction.

Possibly – but what is certain is that modern publishing uses either single quotes or double quotes as standard: it's one form or the other for all purposes, then the alternative form for quotes within quotes.

1   Quote marks are used for direct speech and also for quotations from printed material:

He said: 'You're crazy.'
Jane Austen once wrote: 'An annuity is a very serious business.'

2   Where phrases or single words are quoted, punctuation is generally outside the quote marks:

He said she was 'crazy'.

In the US (but not in Britain) commas are invariably inside the quote marks:

She was 'crazy,' he said. (US)
She was 'crazy', he said. (Britain)

3   But in both Britain and the US commas are inside the quote marks when they end quoted sentences:

'You're crazy,' she was told. (Britain)
'You're crazy,' she was told. (US)

4 Where successive paragraphs are in quotes, each one starts with a quote mark but only the last one has a concluding quote mark:

He said: 'You're crazy. I can't believe you did that. What do you think you're doing? What's going to happen next?

'And another thing – why are we wasting our time arguing with the opposition? Why don't we just go ahead and do things our way?

'I, for one, think we should take the initiative, stop messing about and make them listen to us for a change.'

5 Quotes within quotes take the alternative form:

He said: 'I really meant to say, "I'm sorry." ' (Britain)
He said: "I really meant to say, 'I'm sorry.' " (US)

6 Quote marks are used for the titles of articles, songs, stories, book chapters, episodes in TV series etc:

'The Necklace' is one of Maupassant's best short stories.

7 Quote marks are used to refer to particular words or phrases:

The plural of 'mongoose' is 'mongooses' not 'mongeese'.
In Britain a sidewalk is called a 'pavement'.
'Use your loaf' is rhyming slang (loaf of bread – head).

In these examples the quote marks are used neutrally – there is no comment implied.

8 When people use quotes to distance themselves from an expression they use, suggesting that it's beneath them, they are said to be using 'scare quotes':

Some 'cowboys' failed to fix my roof.

Used like this, scare quotes say to the reader: don't blame me for using this expression.

Round brackets – *see* **Brackets**
Scare quotes – *see* **Quote marks**

Semicolon

1   Use semicolons between sentences, with or without a conjunction, as a longer pause than a comma and a shorter one than a full stop:

The rumour was that the king was dead; the people believed it.

There will be an inquest of course; but the matter will not end there.

2   Use semicolons to separate long items in a list, particularly if the items themselves need further punctuation by commas:

Punctuation marks include the full stop, which is the strongest stop; the semicolon, which is weaker; and the comma, which is weakest of all.

Slash, bar, diagonal, oblique, shilling mark, solidus, stroke, virgule

The slash (/), pedantically forward slash, also bar, diagonal, oblique, shilling mark, solidus, stroke and virgule (particularly among US academics), is used:

1   To mark alternatives:

You can have fish and/or meat.

(You have three choices: fish or meat or fish and meat.)

2   In website addresses:

http://journalists.org/

3   In dates:

He was born on 25/12/01.
(for 25 December)

Or in the US:

He was born on 12/25/01.
(for December 25)

4   In abbreviations, eg to mean per:

The rate is £100/day.

5   And also in the short form of 'care of' in addresses:

Smith c/o Jones

6   At the end of lines of verse laid out like prose:

I have eaten your bread and salt, / I have drunk your water and wine.

Solidus – *see* **Slash**
Square brackets – *see* **Brackets**
Star – *see* **Asterisk**
Tilde – *see* **Accents**
Umlaut – *see* **Accents**

Underlining

Underlining in written text was the traditional way of drawing attention to certain words, eg for emphasis or quotation; it was the equivalent (for those who were not professional typesetters) of setting material in italic type. Now that the standard word-processing package includes italic and bold type, underlining has become what it always was for the professionals – an extra way of marking headings etc.

Virgule – *see* **Slash**

Further reading

The first book on your shelf, even before this one, should be a good, up-to-date dictionary, eg one of those published by Oxford University Press, Chambers or Collins.

There's also a specialist dictionary catering for everyone (whether amateur, student or professional) who takes their writing seriously, called the **New Oxford Dictionary for Writers and Editors**. It concentrates on queries and problems, whether common or abstruse. Several newspapers publish expanded versions of the stylebooks used by their journalists, covering the various aspects of English usage and publishing practice. I particularly recommend **Guardian Style** by David Marsh.

The best general reference book on English usage is the third edition of HW Fowler's **Modern English Usage**, revised and updated by the distinguished lexicographer Robert Burchfield. This is the standard work. Other useful books in the same field are the **Longman Guide to English Usage** by Sidney Greenbaum and Janet Whitcut and **Mind the Gaffe** by RL Trask. The American classic to set beside Fowler is the (much shorter) book by William Strunk and EB White, **The Elements of Style**; a modern American equivalent is **That or Which, and Why** by Evan Jenkins.

Most of these books are organised alphabetically for easy reference, as are Bill Bryson's **Troublesome Words** and my own **Quite Literally**. This includes longer versions of some of the entries in the Problem words chapter.

The linguistics academic David Crystal is the author of various books on English including two useful ones on grammar, **Rediscover Grammar** and **Making Sense of Grammar**. Most people will not need a separate book on spelling – and apart from dictionaries, such books are rare. Punctuation guides, on the other hand, proliferate. The best of them is the **Penguin Guide to Punctuation**, by RL Trask. The celebrated **Eats, Shoots & Leaves** is best seen as an entertaining read round the subject rather than a guide.

Further reading

Bryson, Bill, *Troublesome Words*, Viking, 2001

Burchfield, Robert, *The New Fowler's Modern English Usage* (third edition), OUP, 1996

Crystal, David, *Making Sense of Grammar*, Pearson Longman, 2004

— *Rediscover Grammar* (third edition), Pearson Longman, 2004

Greenbaum, Sidney, and Whitcut, Janet, *Longman Guide to English Usage*, Penguin, 1996

Hicks, Wynford, *Quite Literally: Problem Words and How to Use Them*, Routledge, 2004

Jenkins, Evan, *That or Which, and Why*, Routledge, 2007

Marsh, David, *Guardian Style*, Guardian Books, 2007

Ritter, RM (ed and comp), *New Oxford Dictionary for Writers and Editors*, OUP, 2005

Strunk, William, and White, EB, *The Elements of Style* (fourth edition), Allyn and Bacon, 2000

Trask, RL, *Penguin Guide to Punctuation*, Penguin, 1997

— *Mind the Gaffe: The Penguin Guide to Common Errors in English*, Penguin, 2001

Truss, Lynne, *Eats, Shoots & Leaves*, Profile, 2003